Fish Tales
For Heaven's Sake!

The Collected Parables Of An Alaskan Harbor

Fish Tales
For Heaven's Sake!

The Collected Parables Of An
Alaskan Harbor

Kathy J. Peterson

Mountain Ministries
Sitka, Alaska

Library of Congress Catalog Number: 96-94519

PHOTOGRAPHY
Front Cover: ANB Harbor, Sitka, Alaska
Back Cover: Salmon trolling in Sitka Sound

* * * * *

Illustrations by Mark Bartlett
Cover Design by Alison Caputo
Photography by Linda K. Cook

* * * * *

Published by Mountain Ministries
P.O. Box 6131
Sitka, Alaska 99835

ISBN 0-9653402-5-2

First Edition

Printed in the United States of America

Dedicated to Alaska's fishing families
(and to one very special Skipper...)

"Those who go down to the sea in ships,
Who do business on great waters;
They have seen the works of the Lord,
And His wonders in the deep."

"Fairweather Fisherman"

CONTENTS

Acknowledgments

I would like to thank Sharon Romine at Creative Connections for her willingness to publish these stories originally as *"Parables From The Harbor"* in her weekly shopper, the Sitka Soup.

Thanks, too, to local readers and friends for their encouraging support. A special thank-you to Amy Johnson for her thoughtful note suggesting that the parables belong in a book.

I would also like to express my appreciation to Ellen Grant for a timely and insightful review of the manuscript.

Finally, I want to acknowledge three talented Sitka artists – Mark Bartlett, Alison Caputo, and Linda Cook – whose contributions have dressed up the Fish Tales immeasurably.

Preface

"North – the word's a magnet, I swear it! For two years that little word dragged my husband and me all over Seattle. It led us into boat yards and gear shops. It pulled us downtown to haggle with maritime bankers. And finally, it lured us into the wheel house of a fishing boat and towed us off to Alaska...."

Twelve years later, we're still here – loyal captives of the north country — catching salmon, halibut, and an occasional flight back home. We've fished Alaska's waters long enough now to realize that North is the place where stories really *happen*. Stories with white-knuckle plots and surprise endings; strong characters and inspiring settings.

We've had close encounters with whales as big as a house, porpoises by the hundreds, and sleek grizzlies on the beach that made us gulp in astonished wonder. My journals are full of real-life accounts of boat fires, mayday calls, and hair-raising ocean storms. Recorded, too, are priceless recollections of our family's sometimes reluctant adjustment to life at sea in a one-room boat cabin. (We laugh now, but it hasn't always been so funny!)

Intermingled throughout these writings are occasional thoughts and insights about God that have come to mind during our stay in this rugged place. In a business where the ocean plays for keeps and life-and-death struggles are just part of a day's work, I found myself thinking of Him more and more.

Somewhere along the line I started noticing striking parallels between our experiences and these theological ponderings that lent themselves to combining and retelling as parables. The sea lion that spent most of a day nabbing salmon from our trolling lines became the Devourer – a familiar, even universal, nuisance forever nibbling at the edge of our wallet. The skeptic who told us we'd never make a go of it in Alaska was tagged the Dream Slayer. Surely anyone who's ever had a wild or unlikely goal has had a run-in with this gloomy fellow.

Then there were the fishers themselves – the tenacious men and women who own and operate the work-boats in Alaska's fishing fleet. The stories they told and the lessons they taught us first-hand about faith, and persistence, and life in general could fill a hundred books. In the parables, their varied personalities gradually blended together over time into one unforgettable character: the Skipper – without a doubt life's most entertaining, inspiring, and unbeatable Top Dog!

For the past several years, these private scribblings have been published locally in a neighborhood shopper, mainly for the benefit of the fishing families we've come to know. The goal was to put into words the essence of their unique lifestyle, while at the same time sharing with them the bit of light that has come from my studies.

Reader response has confirmed, however, that Devourers, Dream Slayers, and Top Dogs aren't the private domain of the harbor. Alaskan fishermen aren't the only ones facing struggles, maydays, and uncertain futures. In these sometimes dark days, who among us couldn't use a little more light?

"Coming Aboard"

CHAPTER ONE

JACK AND THE BOX
(AND OTHER FISHING FRIENDS)

Every fisher has a tale to tell. There's Jack and Martin, Lisa and Mary, Charlie, Harry, and our good friend, Jim. The names may be fictitious but if you have time to listen to their stories, you'll find a grain of truth in each one. That's how it is with a parable. *"He who has ears to hear, let him hear...."*

Martin Gets Lucky

"I feel lucky! Oooohh, I feel lucky...."
Martin hummed as he tied up the last plug.
"There! Hey, man, I am *ready!"*

A king salmon opening was scheduled
for the next morning, and yes — for once,
Martin was ready. Maybe in the past he
didn't have it together, but this year would
be different. He happily set his alarm clock
and dropped right off to sleep.

In what only seemed like minutes, the
alarm sang out. Martin opened one eye just
enough to see that it was still pitch black.
He lay in his bunk, listening to his neighbors
pulling anchor. Shouldn't he be getting up,
too? "Aw, what's the hurry? No way those
fish can see in the dark!" With that, he
pulled a fluffy pillow over his head and
drifted back into a delicious early morning
snooze.

Hours later, Martin woke again to find
himself alone in the anchorage. "Well, guess
I'd better run on out there and get my share!
The big boys should have 'em pretty well
rounded up by now."

He fired up the engine and cranked on the radio to check in with his buddy. "Hey Sam! So give me the scoop! How deep ya fishin'? What's the hot gear?"

"*That you, Martin?*" Sam sounded excited. "*Hey fella, you just missed one hot king bite! I must have a hundred, I swear! It's dropped off to nothing now, though. Sorry, friend, but I'm afraid your timing's 'way off.*"

Very often, success is critically tied to timing. So many of the opportunities God brings into our lives are keyed to a specific moment in time. That moment comes – and then it goes. We deceive ourselves if we think we have all the time in the world to do the things He has for us to do.

So here's the deal, Martin. You might be ready. You might even "feel lucky". But man, you have to be on time!

* * * * *

"*But sanctify Christ as Lord in your hearts, always being ready to make a defense to everyone who asks you to give an account of the hope that is in you, yet with gentleness and reverence.*"
I PETER 3: 15

The Dream Slayer

Jim checked the fish plant message board for his shift assignment. "*Yes!* I'm on the hoist today!" Grabbing his rain gear, he scrambled down the stairs to start unloading the fishing boats.

It wasn't that Jim liked the work at the fish plant so much. It's just that he was *crazy* about boats, and the job gave him a chance to get close to them. He knew the skippers by name, and the stories they told stirred him deep. Oh, what he wouldn't give to be a fisherman!

The first boat to pull up to the hoist that morning was long and sleek, painted shiny black with flawless turquoise trim. Her name stood out on the bow like a delicate gem. She was a Satin Doll, for sure.

"Look at that beauty!" Jim usually kept his thoughts to himself, but the sight of her was just too much. "Someday, by golly, I'm going to have me a boat like that."

His boss overheard and laughed tiredly. "Get real," he mumbled. "In all your life you'll never earn the bucks for that one. Besides, just look at yourself. Puny little body! Skinny little arms! If I were you, I'd just stick with what you've got going here and be satisfied."

Tell me, do you recognize that voice? If you've ever had a wild or unlikely dream, you probably know it all too well – the sluggish voice of the *Dream Slayer*. Often he speaks out of the mouths of those closest to us. Our supervisor, coworkers, even family and good friends. "Give it up," he says heavily. "It'll never be. Go back to sleep and forget it."

So what do you do when this stifling messenger speaks up? How should you react? Jesus had some simple advice: "Expect it," He told His disciples, "and *ignore it!*"

Just because the people around you aren't wildly supportive, it's no reason to abandon your dreams. Listen instead to the encouraging voice of God – and get going!

* * * * *

Jesus said to them, "A prophet is not without honor except in his home town and among his own relatives and in his own household." MARK 6: 4

Fire in the Cabin!

Live and let live, they say. You take care of your stuff and I'll take care of mine. But is it ever right to sit back and let your neighbor's boat burn?

Mary enjoyed the harbor in the morning. She woke early just to soak up the quiet. Even when the place was choked with boats, it had a delicious privacy about it. Everybody pretty much tended to their own business.

One Saturday morning, no different than any other, she sat at the galley table reading the paper and watching the gulls argue over breakfast. Once in awhile her eyes swept across the crowd of troll poles and masts. That's when she spotted the smoke – a white wisp at first, and then black billowy clouds, shot through with bright flames!

Dressed only in sweats and stocking feet, Mary pitched out the back door and sprinted down the dock.

"Fire! *Boat fire!*" she screamed. Sleepy neighbors came on the run, scrambling for hoses and buckets. Mary didn't recognize the boat, and she didn't have any idea who the skipper was. But that didn't stop her from vaulting the rail and banging on the wheel-house door. "Wake up! Wake *up! Your boat's afire!"*

I guess you know it was one grateful guy who stopped by her cabin to say thanks a few hours later. He owed her his life, he said.

This little incident makes me think of the times I've been tempted to interfere in someone else's life when it looked to me like they were in trouble. Don't you sometimes wonder when it's right to butt in? I don't know about you, but I'm pretty cautious about crossing that line. A person can get burned.

Still, once in awhile I get to thinking I smell smoke. That's when I ask myself: How high do the flames have to get before I say something?

* * * * *

"If any among you strays from the truth, and one turns him back, let him know that he who turns a sinner from the error of his way will save his soul from death, and will cover a multitude of sins." JAMES 5: 19, 20

Jack And The Box

Normally Cape Edgecumbe is an easy place to fish. Nothing tricky about the drag. The ocean floor is smooth, and all the boats in the fleet troll back and forth along the beach in a generally accepted pattern. All the boats, that is, except *Jack's*. That's one guy who seems to have his own set of rules....

No matter where you steer, it won't be long before Jack will have you on a collision course. First he shows up on your starboard, so you adjust your course to give him some room. Next thing you know, he's coming straight at you. Nothing to do but break out of the drag and circle in behind him. About the time you make a move, he'll decide to make a turn, too – right over your float bags!

All around him, you can see the other skippers scrambling to stay out of his way. Gear gets tangled and lines get kinked. The radio burns with curses and insults flung in all directions. It's a real mess, I'll tell you.

One problem with Jack is that he's trying to run his boat all by himself, without an auto-pilot. He stays on the wheel for awhile, sure, but then he runs to the troll pit to check his lines. Where that boat goes when he's not steering is anybody's guess.

What ticks me off is that I know for a fact Jack does have a brand-new auto-pilot on board — top quality, too. I saw it myself, still in the box and stowed under the captain's chair.

"Hey," I had asked, "When did you get *that?*"

"The pilot? Oh, it came with the boat, actually. Practically a gift...."

"*Really?*" (I was incredulous. Jack had owned the boat for five years!) "So how come you never hooked it up?"

"Aw, too much trouble. I'd have to rewire everything on the panel, ya know. I probably couldn't figure how to work the blamed thing, anyhow."

I thought of all the close calls, and all the ruined gear. You know, it made me half mad. What good is a piece of equipment like that if you never take it out of the box and use it?

* * * * *

"Do not neglect the spiritual gift within you."
I Timothy 4:14

23

Lisa

Lisa rewound the tape for what must have been the tenth time. By now she knew every painful note by heart, but still she listened again. It was all part of a torturous ritual that followed her every performance.

Earlier that day, she had played a flute solo for the annual Blessing of the Fleet. It shouldn't have been a big deal, but Lisa considered herself to be a professional. Every public appearance was significant, regardless of the occasion or size of the audience. Besides, her dad had asked her to do this. These were his friends, and so it mattered especially that she do well.

The tape was all that remained of her brief part in the ceremony. Others had gone on about their day, the moment long since forgotten. But not Lisa. For her, this record would be added to a growing stack of evidence in a never-ending assessment of her musical worth. She would play it until she was sick of it, searching critically for the slightest flaw and agonizing over each she found. The number she had selected for today was overly difficult, and the results were far from perfect. No amount of replaying would change her personal verdict: *Not good enough.* But then, it never was.

You probably know Lisa – or someone much like her. She's what we call a perfectionist. For these people, feelings of self worth are critically tied to performance. They drive themselves compulsively to measure up to an impossible standard, then ruthlessly evaluate the outcome. Their conclusion is always the same: *"Could have been better. Should have tried harder. Not good enough!"*

How the heart of God must ache for Lisa! Who but He can understand the complexity of her motives? The compelling need to get it right, and the torment of always falling short? Surely only He can see the hurtful chains that bind her to this record of past mistakes. And who but God can set her free?

* * * * *

"But when the time came for the kindness of God our Savior to appear, then He saved us – not because we were good enough to be saved, but because of His kindness and pity..." TITUS 3: 4, 5 (TLB)

Follow That Boat!

"Cheechako!" Much as Harry hated the nickname, it fit him to a tee. He was a Southeast newcomer, for sure, and it showed. But that didn't stop him from enjoying his new Alaskan home. Right off the bat he bought a small pleasure boat, and every weekend he set out to explore the complex network of islands near town.

Harry's boat didn't have a radar, so each Friday he just followed other boats into the meandering channels. And each Sunday evening he followed them back home again. It was this navigational strategy that found Harry motoring along deep in the heart of the island maze when the fog hit – sudden and thick as pea soup.

Harry scanned the gray haze for any sign of the boat he'd been tailing. "I think I see his running lights. *Yes!* Look out, fella, I'm closing in!" He moved in close, all right, literally hugging the guy's stern. Nothing to do now but let the boat up front take him home.

Minutes later they came to a fork in the channel. The lead boat turned up the left branch, with Harry right behind. Soon there were more splits. Right, left, right. "Gotta stay close! Just stay close!"

Suddenly Harry noticed the bottom coming up. Twenty fathoms. Ten. Two! He jerked back on the throttle, as the boat out ahead came to an abrupt halt. By now he could make out the shoreline all around. Well, what do you know? A dead end!

Harry hollered to the skipper in the lead. "Hey, where *are* we, man? I don't have a radar!" The skipper shrugged. *"Don't ask me, buddy. I don't have one, either!"*

It's important to have leaders, isn't it? (Especially when you're a Cheechako.) But who you choose for a leader is mighty important, too. It's a fact that not every person out front really knows where he's going. It's also a fact that not every channel will take you home.

* * * * *

"A blind man cannot guide a blind man, can he? Will they not both fall into a pit?" LUKE 6: 39

Three Men In A Tub

Charlie leaned back in the captain's chair and listened as Joe and Tom discussed their idea: Now that individual fishing quotas were here, why not pool their shares and fish together? Rather than paying big bucks to three separate crews, they could do the work themselves and split the profits. A joint venture among three old friends! How could they lose?

It sounded good, but Charlie had a question. "So tell me, who's going to be the *skipper?*" Each man had a boat of his own, you see, and each man was used to running things *his* way.

Joe laughed. "Well, that oughta be obvious. We'll be using my boat – so I guess that makes me the boss!"

Charlie winced. Joe was a lot of fun to have around, but he tended to disappear when the work got boring or hard. After all, that's what he had a crew for!

"Get serious," countered Tom. "I've got the most shares, and I've always had the biggest crew."

Oh boy, thought Charlie. A workaholic skipper! Tom had a lot of quota, all right, but he'd just about killed himself and his crew getting it.

Charlie left his two buddies to their squabble and moved outside onto the back deck. Just the thought of being cooped up with these guys on a boat for days at a time made his skin crawl. "Man, if I could do the job myself, I wouldn't even have a crew. Just let me be my own boss."

Let's face it, joint ventures are hard to pull off. Even when everybody agrees it's the best way to go, things start breaking down when it comes to giving up personal control. And to top things off, it seems like God inevitably pairs us up with people who drive us nuts! But the fact is that in spite of personal differences and personality quirks, we need each other. God knows, there are some jobs that just won't get done unless we row together.

* * * * *

"God has placed the members, each one of them, in the body, just as He desired. And the eye cannot say to the hand, 'I have no need of you.'" I Corinthians 12: 18, 21

All Shapes and Sizes

When we started earning
          Our wage on the sea,
The fishermen weren't like
          I thought they would be.
I thought they'd be pressed
          From a similar mold,
From Norske and Swede
          Fishing families of old.

The joke was on me
          When I first met a few;
They came in all sizes
          And all ages, too!
Tall ones and short ones;
          Seasoned and green.
Mellow and laid-back;
          Hard-driven and lean.

Some skippers were women,
          With boats of their own.
Some fished with their families
          And some worked alone.
Tlingets and Haidas
          And Eskimos, too;
Been fishing a long time
          Before me and you!

They call themselves fishers;
                    They're proud of the name!
In many ways different,
                    Yet somehow the same.
What draws them together?
                    It just well may be
Their adventurous spirit
                    And love for the sea.

When Jesus went scouting
                    For fishers of men,
This group was the logical
                    Place to begin.
He went to the beach
                    For a brief interview,
And when He came back,
                    He had picked out a few.

No wonder the people
                    Who still bear His name
Are uniquely different,
                    Yet so much the same!
What draws us together?
                    It just has to be
The work of His Spirit
                    Inside you and me.

* * * * *

"God gives us many kinds of special abilities, but it is the same Holy Spirit who is the source of them all.... It is the same God who does the work in and through all of us who are His." I COR. 12: 4, 6 (TLB)

31

"Travelling Chums"

CHAPTER TWO

"PARDON ME, SKIPPER..."

Everybody knows the Skipper is Top Dog in this business. Don't think he doesn't feel the pressure, too! Then there's his crew – sometimes good, sometimes bad – but always willing to give the Skipper a run for his money. Skippers and deckhands – they're a special breed.

Top Dog

Out on the fishing grounds, the Skipper is Top Dog. He hollers and spits and calls the shots. Every fish that comes aboard belongs to him – another mark on the wall, another point on the score board.

At the end of the day, when he asks, *"So how'm I doing?"* he can look in the fish hold and answer his own question. *"Hmmmm... Not bad!"* Yes sir, out on the water (away from the crowds!) the Skipper is Number One.

Unfortunately, once in awhile the Top Dog has to go to shore. Back in the harbor, he's going to run into a hundred more just like himself. And they'll all strut around the docks, asking each other the same question: *"So how'm I doing?"*

But, of course, they don't put it quite that way. It goes more like this: "So how'd *you* do?" And everybody knows what's really being asked here: How'd you do in comparison to *me*? Did I win? Did I lose?

Winners and losers. Consciously or not, we're all out there competing at every level, playing little games of one-on-one a million times a day. Our pockets are stuffed with the score cards. I'm sure you know how it goes:

We meet on the street. In between cheerful greetings, I check out your stuff and you check out mine. There's the car, the salary, the kids' grades, the house. After saying goodbye, we both walk away, silently totaling the scores. *"So how'm I doing?"* we ask. *"Did I win? Did I lose?"*

I wonder why we do this comparing thing, anyway? Why isn't it good enough to just do the best we can and be satisfied? In the end, there's really only one game that's going to matter. And I suspect that coming out on top won't have anything to do with scores at all.

* * * * *

"For by grace you have been saved by faith; and that not of yourselves, it is a gift of God; not as a result of works, that no one should boast." Ephesians 2: 8, 9

Candy Land

This was it for Danny – his moment of glory. He'd been to the boat show and come away with a brand new troller. Now he was about to bring her in for a show of another kind: his Grand Entrance into home port.

All the way home, the new skipper had fantasized about how it would be. He'd be up on the flying bridge, in full control. The sun would dance on the rigging and the fresh paint would glisten. Everyone in the harbor would stop their work to admire the sight. Over and over, he savored the sweet taste of it.

The only sour-ball in his candy land daydream was that this was an awful lot of boat to handle, especially around the docks. So just to play it safe, he had a couple of buddies stationed out back, each armed with buoys and instructions from Danny to protect the paint (and his ego!) at all personal cost.

Now everyone knows that the measure of a good skipper is his ability to put his boat where he wants it – on the *first* try. Danny's friends were about to learn, though, that what this often means for a rookie is that as soon as he can manage to get it anywhere near the dock, he's going to let off with a desperate scream: "Jump! *Jump!!*" Then it'll be up to the crewman with the longest legs to make a flying leap across an ever-widening span and save his leader from disgrace.

A person can't help but sympathize with Danny. Who doesn't fantasize about great performances and totally brilliant finishes? But can you see a problem here? What about motives? And values? Funny how life's little chances at personal glory can give these a subtle twist. Suddenly even our best friends become expendable pawns, either helping or hindering our glorious moment.

Seems, too, that the more public the performance, the more susceptible we are. It takes a lot of character to forego the ego binge and stay focused on the job at hand. Hmmm... Maybe *that* should be the measure of a good skipper!

* * * * *

"It is not good to eat much honey,
Nor is it glory to search out one's own glory."
PROVERBS 25: 27

Go or No-Go?

"For the outside waters, Dixon Entrance to Cape Fairweather, small craft advisory; winds south 20 knots. Outlook: showers; winds southeast twenty five knots."

The Skipper turned from the radio to face his waiting crew. "How 'bout it, Skip? We goin' out?"

The weather can turn on a dime up here, in spite of the reports, and every fishing trip boils down to this moment of decision. Go or no-go? It was his call.

It isn't a question of right or wrong. To head out or postpone a trip is more a matter of wisdom or foolishness. A wise skipper knows to fear the weather. He's lost too many friends not to. But then there's the thing about the crew....

Suppose the Skipper lets his fear of the weather win out. "Nope, not today," he says. "Too risky." Sure as anything, later that day the wind will back off and the water will lay down flat as a lake. He'll watch the crew grumble among themselves about their empty pockets. Up at the bar they'll laugh behind his back and call him a coward.

What if, on the other hand, his fear of their disapproval pressures him into going out against his better judgment? I'll tell you what, if the weather blows up and the gear busts off and the crew gets a good scare, they'll curse that skipper to his face and call him a dangerous fool.

To be overly concerned with what others might think or say about us is what the Bible calls "the fear of man". And the fear of man, it goes on to say, brings a snare. It traps us into doing things we don't believe in, just to avoid being criticized or laughed at. It makes us take foolish chances. It holds its hand over our mouths when we know we should be speaking up.

One thing's for sure. When it starts affecting the wisdom of our choices, the fear of man is downright dangerous.

* * * * *

"Many even of the rulers believed in Him, but because of the Pharisees they were not confessing Him, lest they should be put out of the synagogue; for they loved the approval of men rather than the approval of God." JOHN 12: 42

A New Approach

"During times of change, experience may be your worst enemy." So says the sign on the message board at the fish plant. Every time I read it, I'm reminded of our deck hand, Jake.

Jake was, without a doubt, the most reliable help we'd ever had. He had experience, all right, and he stuck with the job. You'd see him in the troll pit for hours, first running the deep and float-bag lines on the starboard, then checking the port-side lines. After he'd cleaned whatever salmon had come aboard, he started the whole process over. This was his unchanging routine and he kept at it, day in and day out.

Whenever we pulled into the harbor, Jake had another routine that set in. Just as the boat nosed into the stall, he could be counted on to come flying out of the cabin to help with the ropes. With one hand on the rail he'd be over the side and on the dock, ready to catch the bow line when I gave it a toss.

Now I have to tell you, the Skipper is pretty predictable, too. He *always* moors the boat bow first, with the dock on the port-side. So don't ask me why it was that one fateful day he decided to *back* into the stall instead, which put the dock on the *starboard*.

I can still see Jake boiling out of that cabin on a dead run, heading for the port side. Before I could even open my mouth, he was into his dismount – one hand on the rail and two feet suspended (only briefly!) in mid-air over the water. The look of shock on his face said it all: *"During times of change..."*

Experience alone doesn't guarantee success. Like Jake, I'm finding that what worked yesterday doesn't always work so well today. Though God Himself has not and does not change, the world in which we live has changed radically. As we consider the gifts and talents He's given us, it might not hurt to think about trying a new approach. People who say we have to keep doing the same old things over and over in the same old way just might turn out to be "all wet".

* * * * *

"Sing to the Lord a new song."
PSALM 149: 1

Spring Cleaning

The Skipper cringed. "Boy now, that's a sight, isn't it?" The crane hoisted his boat ashore and motored across the yard. From where he stood, all he could see was a mass of seaweed and long strings of kelp trailing from the hull.

The view only got worse as he walked closer. Mussels and barnacles crusted every inch below the water line. No wonder the transducers hadn't been working. What a mess!

Now the question was, how to clean her up? The Skipper looked at the little spray washer he'd rented and laughed. No way! He went below in the hold, rummaged around for awhile, and came up with an ice scraper – a heavy duty job with a shovel handle and a six-inch steel blade.

Then he just started shaving that big whale's belly, scraping and jabbing from the bow to the stern. It took him most of a day, but little by little the crust peeled off.

The next morning he was back at it early, toting the biggest washer in town. The water hit the steel hull in sharp spears, blasting off the last of the garbage and leaving a clean, polished surface.

The paint went on next, in long, smooth strokes of fresh red. It felt good going on. Looked great, too. "I'll tell you," he mused, "This is still one good boat!"

You know, I'd be willing to bet all that debris didn't grow on our friend's boat overnight. No, life's garbage is more likely to build up on you a little at a time. A trace of bitterness and resentment here, some anger and hurt feelings there. Over time you gradually start to notice things just aren't working quite right. It's like your soul's all crusted over with some kind of residue.

Maybe the lesson here is that it's not enough to keep everything cleaned and painted above the water line. Maybe once in awhile a person needs to get with God and schedule a "haul-out".

* * * * *

"Be gracious to me, O God, according to Thy lovingkindness. According to the greatness of Thy compassion, blot out my transgressions. Wash me thoroughly from my iniquity, and cleanse me from my sin." PSALM 51: 1, 2

Double Booked

The boss signed on an extra man
        To help me bait the gear;
But every time I turned around,
        The guy would disappear!
He seemed so well-intentioned.
        (Oh, he would have *liked* to help!)
But every job we had, I wound up
        Doing by myself.

I got a little curious.
        ("Where does that deck hand go?")
So one day I went scouting
        Through the harbor, row by row.
Was I surprised to find him –
        Working on *another* boat!
"I'm almost finished here," he said,
        "And then I'll help *you* out."

We both agreed that after lunch
        We'd start to chop the bait.
But just like all the other times,
        He showed up hours late.
"I would have been here sooner,
        But I promised Joe and Tim
That this would be the afternoon
        I'd do some things for them."

About that time the Skipper came
   To see how much we'd done.
"How come it takes two deck hands now
   To do the work of one?!"
His scowling face got dark and red;
   His hands were clenched in fists.
(I'd seen the Skipper mad before,
   But never quite like this!)

He brushed me off and backed the other
   Deck hand to the door.
"I've been around awhile, kid.
   You bet I know the score.
You've got a schedule problem
   That you may have overlooked;
I'm not about to pay a guy
   Whose life is double-booked!"

"Dear Lord," I sometimes grandly pray,
   "I give my life to You."
"Your life?" He answers, *"You've already*
   Got too much to do.
You're struggling now to keep up with
   The hectic pace you live.
Until you trim your schedule back,
   You have no 'life' to give!"

Diminishing Returns

One more tub of gear
    And then it's Celebration Time;
We had an awesome season –
    Loads of fish on every line.
The Skipper's at the bank now,
    Getting everybody's share.
Just pay us off in thousands –
    Stacks of hundreds! We don't care!

Hey, here he comes. (I wonder why
    He always seems to scowl?
If I had that guy's money,
    I'd be doing handstands now!)
"Good job," he says. *"You guys were great;*
    Best crew I ever chose.
I wish the checks were bigger,
    But that's just the way it goes."

Hey, just a second, Sir.
    I think your calculator's broke.
Such tiny little numbers!
    Man, is this some kind of joke?
The way I had it figured
    I'd be getting fifteen grand,
So I could buy a car
    And take a trip to Disneyland!

"Well, son, this is the hardest thing
A deck hand ever learns:
The Economic Lesson
Of Diminishing Returns.
See, every fish we catch out there
Is smaller than you think,
And by the time we get to town,
The whole load starts to shrink."

"The fish plant takes a hefty share
For buying in the round.
We had a lot of gear loss
When that big boat set us down.
Bait and fuel cost money,
And your groceries were the best.
I subtract it all and then
The boat gets half the rest."

Well that's just great – a thousand bucks!
So maybe Dad was right.
Don't fix your hopes on money;
It can vanish overnight.
Chasing after riches
Leads to emptiness and greed.
"In God we trust," Dad used to say.
"He'll take care of your need."

"For wealth certainly makes itself wings, like an
eagle that flies toward the heavens." PROVERBS 23: 5

Pardon Me, Skipper...

"Pardon me, Skipper.
    Do you need a bigger crew?
I was born on the water
    And there's *nothin'* I can't do.
They know me pretty well
    On all the high-line boats out west;
I've put in fifteen seasons,
    Always workin' for the best!"

"Well, you're a little young
    To make the claim you've done it all;
Your hands seem awful soft to me
    And you look pretty small.
But I'm a crewman short
    And I'll be leaving town today;
The halibut are waitin';
    Boy, you're gonna earn your pay!"

Twenty hours later,
    They were hauling fish on deck.
"Uh, sir, I need some dinner –
    And I didn't get my break!
I'm sure not used to fishing
    When the water's rough and deep;
And I'm not worth a lick
    If I don't get my beauty sleep!"

The Skipper's voice was even,
     But his eyes were stern and cold.
"Hey, I suggest you clean these fish
     And get 'em in the hold.
If I remember right, son,
     You're supposed to be the star;
There's more to catching halibut
     Than talking at the bar!"

I hear God's got a vacancy;
     He's looking for some crew.
The time is growing short,
     And there's a lot of work to do.
But He needs more than *talkers*;
     (Man, there's plenty on the loose.)
What He needs now are *"do-ers"* –
     People willing to produce.

John and Peter left their boats
     To follow after Him;
No longer netting salmon,
     They went out to fish for men.
If that's a job you're wanting,
     You might like to come aboard;
But be prepared to earn your pay;
     You're working for the Lord!

* * * * *

*"And He said to them, 'Follow Me, and I will
make you fishers of men.'"* MATTHEW 4: 19

"Sheriffs Sale Leftover"

CHAPTER THREE

TURBULENT TRANSITIONS

Our move to Alaska involved a radical lifestyle change. In some ways you could say we were born again – from dry-land farmers to salt-water fishers. As with any genuine conversion, there was a price to pay.

A Pink Slip Day

They sent the men home early the day the pink slips came out. I was at work when the news came over the radio: The saw mill in our Eastern Washington town was shutting down for good. There'd been rumors, but now the word was official – and final. My husband's job would be going down the tubes with a hundred others.

My boss stopped by my desk as soon as he heard. "So what are you guys going to do? Will you be leaving?" *Leaving? Not if I could help it.* "I don't know," I murmured. "We'll have to wait and see...."

I took the long way home that night, driving down the river road to my parents' farm, then up the other side of the valley toward town. Past my old high school and the church where we'd been married. The last half mile took me along the elementary school grounds – behind the football field and empty bleachers, past my kids' classrooms.

At the end of the street, I slowed the car. There was our house – all new and neat and trim. The lawn was just coming in, thick and green. Newly planted shrubs were taking root. Out back, a tidy garden plot snuggled against the fence. It was a picture of small-town living at its best. Leave this little valley? No way! Pink slip or not, I would figure out a way to stay. I just *had* to.

As it turned out, we did end up moving away. There was no choice, really. Without the mill paycheck, we simply couldn't afford to stay. Eventually the savings ran out and things got tight. Good-bye, nice house. Good-bye, old friends. Mom. Dad. Good-bye....

Once in awhile I think back to those dark days. It's been almost twelve years now. But you know something? Nearly every one of those years has been crammed full with new friends, incredible opportunity, and exciting Alaskan adventures. How much of what we've enjoyed since then do you suppose would have occurred without that dreadful pink slip? So maybe it wasn't really *"The End"* after all. Maybe it was more like the first page of countless new beginnings.

* * * * *

"And we know that God causes all things to work together for good to those who love God, to those who are called according to His purpose." Romans 8: 28

A Sheriff's Sale Leftover

There she sat – a sheriff's sale leftover. We were shopping for our first boat when we found her, discarded and forgotten in the back of a Tacoma boat yard. Everything of value had been stripped: engine, radios, rigging, gear. Nothing left but a hollow shell.

To some folks this might have been a depressing sight. But for us the boat was exactly what we'd been looking for. You could see she'd been a beauty in her day – a forty-two foot wooden troller with good lines and a high bow. While rummaging through the cabin, we came across the original bill of sale for ninety-seven thousand dollars. What a find!

My husband noticed a small hole in the outside cabin wall and mentioned it to the seller. "Yeah, well, she's got a little rot, but she's pretty sound overall." We offered him six thousand and he quickly snapped it up.

A few days later, we pulled out of the Tacoma harbor with our new treasure under tow. (That's another story altogether!) Next stop was the Fishermen's Terminal in Seattle.

For the following two years, we would

pour every spare dime and available minute into restoring her to what she once had been – a proud Alaskan troller.

Devalued, discarded, and discovered. Jesus used this theme over and over in His parables to let people know that God is in the business of restoration. He used word pictures about missing sheep, broken pottery, and lost coins to convey the importance He attaches to a second chance.

Driven by love, God combs the boat yards of life, searching for treasure that others have overlooked. He recognizes potential, He knows the original purchase price, and He is out to buy back that which has been cast aside.

* * * * *

"What woman, if she has ten silver coins and loses one coin, does not light a lamp and sweep the house and search carefully until she finds it?

"And when she has found it, she calls together her friends and neighbors, saying, 'Rejoice with me, for I have found the coin which I had lost!'" LUKE 15: 8, 9

One Rope or Two?

Boat motors quit for a million reasons. Or for *no* reason. If you own a boat, this isn't news to you. The incredible thing is that we put ourselves in the most vulnerable situations, knowing this. Every day! Man, I can think of some times....

It was a beautiful spring day when my husband and his brother decided they would use a tiny pleasure boat to tow our disabled troller from Tacoma to Seattle. We'd bought the boat just the week before. She needed lots of work and money was tight. This would be an inexpensive way to get her to the Fishermen's Terminal for a major overhaul.

My husband was in the troller and his brother was in the little tow boat up front as they slowly made their way out of the harbor and into the channel. Two boats, two skippers, a sturdy tow rope, and one engine. It was a situation under control.

For the guy in the back, there wasn't much to do but relax and enjoy the ride. Soak up the sun, watch the other boats, feel the wind, and dream of faraway places.

A couple hours into the trip, the sound of a sputtering engine cut the daydream short. Both men watched the tow rope go limp. *Oh no! Not here!* Right out in the middle of Puget Sound's busiest shipping lanes! Huge freighters, tugs, and barges — and two little boats dead in the water.

The brothers quickly contacted the Coast Guard and explained their predicament. Would they need an assist vessel? Uh no, actually they would need *two!*

Everybody's got a tow rope tied to one thing or another. It might be a job or a satisfying marriage, a savings account or good health. And most of the time, we motor along pretty well. Sometimes we might even coast a little, and let these things just sort of carry us.

But what do you do when the thing you've been counting on the most cuts out? When you're dead in the water, "who ya gonna call?"

* * * * *

"Some trust in chariots, and some in horses; But we will boast in the name of the Lord our God." PSALM 20: 7

"Just a *Little* Rot..."

Everything I know about rot I learned from our first boat. We knew when we bought her that there was a little rot in the cabin. We'd need a couple sheets of plywood and maybe some fiberglass. No problem! "Pretty sound overall," the eager seller had said. Right....

First day of summer vacation we showed up at the marina, ready to go to work. We had pop and chips and sandwiches and our kids and a few tools. My son cranked up the radio and asked, "Where we gonna start, Dad?"

Our task for that day was to fix a small hole in the rear cabin wall. My husband probed the wall, looking for the end of the rot. I watched as he moved to the port side. His screwdriver sunk into a corner post with sickening ease. "That one'll have to come out." He checked the other studs. Most were in a similar condition.

Next thing I knew he was up on the roof, and he looked grim. "Let's start up here," he said. "It's pretty bad." So off came the flying bridge like an old pirate's hat, exposing leprous-white mold on the wood underneath.

One day stretched into another, as we filled the dumpsters with rotten wood. By the end of the week, there wasn't much cabin left. Now it was my daughter who asked, "Hey, Dad – where are we going to *stop*?!"

So... that's how I learned about rot. I learned that it's not always right out there where you can see it. And that it seems to spread from plank to plank. But mainly I learned that skippers hate it. And they won't start adding good wood until they've torn out all the bad.

The idea of a parable is to look for a heavenly meaning in an earthly story. Do you see any parables here? Can't you just picture God showing up on the job like a new skipper? It's a sure bet that when He gets involved in your life, the rotten stuff is going to go. At first you'll eagerly ask, "Where shall we start?" But after He's been at it awhile, you might wonder, "Where's He going to *stop*?!"

* * * * *

"Create in me a clean heart, O God,
And renew a steadfast spirit within me."
PSALM 51: 10

A Turbulent Transition

"That don't look like no hay rack to me!" The farmer watched my husband weld the final bracing in place.

"Yeah, well, that's what the fishermen call this thing. Now I just need to spool some trolling wire onto these gurdies here, and tie up a few hootchies. Then I'll be in business."

"Gurdies? Hootchies?" The old man shook his head. "I swear, I can't understand half of what you're sayin' any more...."

He eyed our open garage. An A-frame mast assembled the week before sprawled out the door and halfway down the driveway. Stacked around it were buoys and boxes of fishing gear. "I don't know what you're up to," he continued, "but it looks like you need a little lesson in geography. This *is farmin' country*, boy, not a doggone boat yard. And if you think you're gonna catch anything using that steel wire, you've got a lot to learn about fishin' *too!*" With that he slammed the door of his pickup and drove off.

It's no wonder the fellow was perplexed. He was right, after all. We lived in a small rural community where people earned their money in very predictable ways. They farmed hay and raised cattle and, at least until recently, they worked at the local saw mill. It was one of those places where things pretty much stay the same. The change he saw in my husband was bound to generate a little anxiety.

But what our neighbor couldn't see was everything that had led up to the seemingly abrupt conversion. Did he know the depth of hunger for something fresh and new that had sparked it all? Had he wrestled with the self-doubt? Was he there in the private, agonizing moment when the decision was finally made to take a chance? Did his hand sweat when the ink went down on boat loan papers?

No, he didn't know about any of that. All he saw were the traces of transition – the odds and ends of something he didn't understand – and I guess it kind of irritated him a little. But then, more often than not, that's how it is with new things.

* * * * *

"Therefore if anyone is in Christ, he is a new creature; the old things passed away; behold, new things have come." II Cor. 5: 17

Through The Playground Gate

"North" — The word's a magnet, I swear it. For two years, that little word dragged my husband and me all over Seattle. It led us into boat yards and gear shops. It pulled us downtown to haggle with maritime bankers. And finally, it lured us into the wheel house of a fishing boat and towed us off to Alaska.

In the quiet freshness of an early spring morning, we cut the ropes that bound us to home port and started on our very own incredible journey. All went well that first day out. We sang sailing songs and ate dried fish and tried to act like sea captains. Oh yes – we were going *North!*

That night, we anchored in a pocket of islands on the edge of Canadian water. After dinner, I wandered out on deck and studied the far shoreline. We'd been here many times before. It was a favorite family playground. But tomorrow, we would pass through the playground gate and on to unfamiliar places.

The thought of it began to sink in. Where we were going, there would be no more weekend picnics with cousins; no evening visits on the farm; no casual cups of tea with my sister. All of a sudden, North was something more than a word. It was a special kind of pain.

Have you ever felt Jesus' words tug at your heart? "Follow Me!", He urges. "I have an incredible journey all lined out especially for you. Would you like to come along?"

You might be one of those who decides to say yes. If so, you'll find it's great fun getting ready to go. But eventually, it's time to cut the ropes and pull away from the dock. That's when it starts to hit: "Wait a minute, Lord! What about my family? My friends? My home?"

I guess there's a price to pay, isn't there? But when you think about it, where would we be if we never said goodbye? Probably still hanging around some playground, I'll bet.

* * * * *

Jesus said, "Everyone who has left houses or brothers or sisters or father or mother or children or farms for My name's sake shall receive many times as much, and shall inherit eternal life." MATTHEW 19: 29

Space Wars

"Mom, Scotty's in my space!" Space? That's something you're just not going to find in the cabin of a small boat. But try explaining that to two dry-land teenagers on their first trip up the Inside Passage.

The space my daughter referred to was her small bunk, wedged between the captain's chair and the back door. In this tiny area Susan had carefully arranged the contents of a teen survival kit of sorts: headphones and tapes, magazines, a poster, and a bulging bag of essential cosmetics.

My son had the upper bunk. It, too, was cluttered with all earthly possessions thought necessary to sustain life as he knew it. Apparently Scotty's gear was spilling over the sides into his sister's air space, and that was the momentary conflict.

Nothing in their short lives had prepared them for anything like this. Home had always been the wide-open expanse of a small town back yard; private bedrooms were the norm. I'd felt it was my duty to deliver the world to them in bite-sized pieces, with fun flavors and pretty colors. Instinctively they looked to me now in their distress and pleaded, "Mom! *Fix it!*"

Fix it? I'm afraid I had my hands full at that moment, helping their dad fix *other* things, like unemployment and unpaid bills. The mill in our town had closed, and we were out of work. We'd bought a fishing boat with what money we had, and now we were on our way to Alaska.

Fix it? Little did they know I was staring hard into the face of God right then, making a similar plea. For the first time in my kids' lives, there wasn't much I could do to help. It was a bitter dose, I could tell, hard for them to swallow.

It's a right and natural thing for a parent to want to shield their children from life's harsh realities. But you and I both know we can't always come through. I've wondered since then if perhaps an equally important duty in parenting is to teach our kids, as they grow, to look *beyond* Mom and Dad, to One who is able to fix just about anything.

* * * * *

"Let us therefore draw near with confidence to the throne of grace, that we may receive mercy and may find grace to help in time of need." HEBREWS 4: 16

A Maritime Mothers Day

This is the time when we think
        About Mother,
And all of the great things
        She's done in her life.
She's raised the best kids,
        And she's got a good job.
She's a marvelous cook –
        An incredible wife!

She gladly accepts all the gifts
        And the praise.
(It hasn't been easy
        To get the job done!)
But think for a minute
        How Mom's life would differ
If she would have married
        An old fisherman....

The first thing to go would have been
        Her big house.
A fine wooden troller
        Would soon take its place.
Mom thought it was crowded when
        My friends stayed over;
Try raising your brood
        In an eight-by-ten space!

Picture Mom's dresses,
        Her best suit and shoes –
Lovingly cared for
        In long closet rows.

How would she cope
        With the essence of diesel,
Soot stains and mildew
        On favorite clothes?

Mom loves her kitchen –
        A gourmet's delight,
Where every appliance
        Is sparkling and new.
A boat galley? Well, that's a
        Different story.
A stove and an ice chest
        Might just have to do.

Now I know some women
        Who live in the harbor.
I've watched them adapt
        To their home on the sea.
They cook and they sew and they
        Play with their children.
It's family life
        Of the best quality.

So you honor your mom,
        And I'll honor mine.
But let's take a minute
        To 'specially note
Our neighbors at sea
        Who deserve recognition.
God bless the mother
        Who lives on a boat!

"Heading For The Harbour"

CHAPTER FOUR

THE SKIPPER TAKES A WIFE
(AND TWO TEEN-AGED KIDS)

Father, mother, son and daughter, crammed into the wheel house of a little boat for six days at a time. A family fishing venture is a risky undertaking, guaranteed to generate some lasting memories.

Watch Out For The Pinnacles!

The Skipper told me if I would come along for the day, all I would have to do was steer the boat. But now that we were actually at it, it was turning out to be a whole lot more complicated.

"Okay now, just keep her pointed toward the island, see? And keep your speed at three knots, like it says right here. There's lots of other boats out there, so don't be making any sharp turns. Be sure to watch the depth, too, whatever you do. I'll be dragging forty fathoms of gear, so don't let it get any more shallow than that! And I'll tell you right now, there's some dandy pinnacles around here. Don't run me over the top of any, okay?"

I wasn't exactly sure what a pinnacle was, but I nodded in agreement to all that he said.

Keeping the depth right turned out to be a lot harder than it sounded. I found myself steering with one eye on the boats out ahead and the other eye glued to the fathometer. By now the Skipper was in the troll pit, running the gear and tossing non-stop orders in my direction as we wove our way across the uneven ocean floor. *"Too deep! Turn in!"* he would holler. *"Too shallow! Turn out!!"* It was a bit of a challenge.

Just about the time I thought I was getting the hang of it, I noticed the bottom starting to turn up sharply on the fathometer screen. I steered out, expecting to see it drop off. It didn't. Instead, it crept steadily upward, steeper by the second, until it literally shot straight up! *Aauugh! A pinnacle!*

Let's see now, what had the Skipper said? "Steer out, and give it lots of throttle!" *Yes, that's it!* In a single motion, I spun the wheel and slammed the throttle forward. The engine roared and belched black smoke. I checked the screen. Twenty fathoms and still climbing. More throttle! I couldn't imagine what was happening in the troll pit by now, but I just had to look....
[To be continued.]

* * * * *

*"For by Thee I can run upon a troop;
And by my God I can leap over a wall."*
Psalm 18: 29

71

Pinnacles! (Part 2)

Pinnacles! Even now the word stirs me up. I can still see it as though it were yesterday: Hand on the throttle, heart in the throat, and the image of that relentless peak shooting higher and higher up the fathometer screen. Thirty fathoms... twenty... fifteen and still climbing!

Out back, the Skipper bellowed like an angry bull. I dared not look his way, but finally I just had to. Burned in my memory forever will be the picture of that dear man standing in the troll pit – hat shoved back, feet braced, and eyes transfixed in a frozen stare at the sight of his trolling lines (all four of 'em – hootchies, flashers, fish and all!) flying crazily behind the boat. And bringing up the rear of each line was a fifty pound cannon ball, skimming lightly across the water's surface!

The pinnacle crested at an incredible eight fathoms. Then the bottom dropped off as suddenly as it had come up; I backed off the throttle and resumed our course; and the Skipper repaired his gear and got back to fishing. Later that day, he remarked that *just maybe* I had over-reacted a little. The trick to jumping pinnacles, he said, is that you have to trust the physics of the thing. Speed up – raise the gear – skim the top – and back off. That's all there is to it, he said. No need for the panic.

Thinking back ten years to this episode, I have to wonder: What, if anything, would I do differently in that same situation now? Would I be calm? Would I steadily increase the throttle and expertly lift the lines up and over the peak?

"Trust the physics," the Skipper had said. I've jumped enough pinnacles of a different sort since then to admit that this has been one of the hardest lessons for me to learn. To trust that in a crisis there are certain laws that kick in, as dependable as God Himself. To trust that He is committed to my good; that He is working effectively on my behalf. Faith like that doesn't come overnight. But little by little, I'm starting to see what the Skipper was getting at.

* * * * *

"This I know, that God is for me. In God, whose word I praise, In God I have put my trust. I shall not be afraid." Psalm 56: 9, 4

A Woman's Place

A woman's place is in the ice hold. Judy hadn't known this before she started fishing with her husband. But she would soon learn that, at the end of a long day (while skipper and kids lounged in the cabin and waited for supper), it was *her* job to go below and ice the day's catch. Then she could come up and fix their dinner.

Actually, Judy had come to enjoy the cool, quiet dimness of the ice hold. The boat got a little small after a few days at sea, and it was nice just to be alone for awhile. She worked at her own pace, filling each fish with clean ice shavings and stacking them in neat rows like cordwood. Every now and then she would pause to sip a cold soda and ponder the day's events. Her somewhat altered relationship with her skipper/ husband provided plenty to think about!

That's where she was one particular evening when suddenly the lone light bulb above her head went out. There she sat, in absolute dark. *"This must be some kind of 'new deck-hand' joke..."* She waited a few minutes longer, expecting the lights to come on and the laughter to start. After awhile it became obvious that neither was going to happen. Apparently, when her husband had shut down the engine and turned off the radios, he had unthinkingly doused the ice hold lights, too!

Judy let the truth of it sink in. "He forgot me!" She repeated it slowly, heating up with each word. "Here I am, icing his blessed fish and *he...forgot...me...!*"

Seconds later a wild-eyed, rage-crazed woman emerged from one very black ice hold. And I can tell you for a fact that if the skipper had indeed forgotten his wife was aboard, he was very soon reminded!

This story is told for the benefit of all you would-be captains out there who are contemplating a family fishing business. A joint venture with your spouse can be a wonderful experience. But if you want your business to last longer than a single trip, be careful to show a little appreciation. And never, *never* stow your wife in the hold.

* * * * *

"An excellent wife, who can find? For her worth is far above jewels.... Her children rise up and bless her; her husband also, and he praises her." PROVERBS 31: 10, 28

Something Smells!

There we were – father, mother, son and daughter – crammed around the small galley table, reaching and grabbing and wolfing down our supper. It was the peak of the coho season and we'd been at sea for five hectic days. All of us were putting in long, hard hours, up to our elbows in blood and fish slime. Dinner was our only relief, and we ate ravenously.

Our soiled rain gear lay in a heap near the door. Four bloodied pairs of gloves were drying above the stove. We had the windows tightly closed against a steady evening rain, and the heat cranked up on high. (Maybe too high, now that I think about it!)

I was well into my second helping of everything when I noticed it was suddenly very quiet at the table. I looked up just in time to catch my daughter's sharp glare.

"Something *smells* in here," she said flatly. Slowly her accusing scowl turned from one face to another. Then, with an air of anguished finality, she pronounced: "*We* smell!" (I can still hear that plaintive voice.) We *all smell!*"

Her father and little brother exchanged puzzled looks. "Huh! I don't smell anything! Do you?" *"Nope. Not a thing!"* Honest to goodness, up until that moment, I hadn't either. But now that she had pointed it out, there *was* an odor about the place that was distinctively foul. There are certain common standards of decency and cleanliness and (as my daughter then proceeded to inform us) we had gradually fallen 'way below the mark.

It's amazing the things a person can get used to over time. Even the most repulsive situation will stop bothering you if you live around it long enough. Before you know it, you get caught up in the business at hand and don't notice that the standards have been allowed to slip.

Thank heaven that in every generation, God raises up a handful of people who are faithful to remind us when it's time to clean up our act.

* * * * *

"Son of man, I have appointed you a watchman to the house of Israel; whenever you hear a word from My mouth, warn them from Me. Say to them, 'Turn back, turn back from your evil ways!'" EZEKIAL 3:17; 33:11

A Heart of Thanksgiving

"I will bless Thee, O Lord, With a heart of thanksgiving." What do you suppose it means to have a heart of thanksgiving? To me it would have to be the feeling I get every time I step into a steaming hot shower....

I never really thought much about water before we started living on our fishing boat. You turn it on, you let it run, you turn it off. No big deal. But once you've spent a summer at sea – two parents and two teens, six-day trips and a hundred-gallon tank of fresh water – you'll never think about it in quite the same way again.

I hadn't realized until then just how much water it takes to keep teen-aged dignity intact! Tell me, have you ever tried to wash dishes in a twelve-ounce cereal bowl, or shampooed your hair in a spaghetti pan? Catching and cleaning fish is messy business; to this day my kids will tell you that foregoing the full-blown ritual of daily shore-side hygiene was the ultimate sacrifice.

Once a week, we'd head to town to unload and re-ice at the fish plant. While we were there, we took full advantage of the facilities they offered the fishermen, which included a half-dozen shower stalls. Can you picture it? After a week at sea – after metering out water by the cup and fussing over every drop – to come face-to-face with an unlimited supply.

That's when I became aware that my attitude was undergoing a radical change. Turn it on. (*Oh yes!*) Let it run. (*Glory to God!*) I'd see the steam rise and feel my grateful heart rise with it. Such a simple thing. Such a wonderful thing! Fresh, hot water – and lots of it!

To have a heart of thanksgiving speaks of a certain quiet appreciation of the most basic provisions. To be genuinely thankful when God brings these our way. Things like a tasty meal, or a warm coat. Maybe even a steaming hot shower. Yes, indeed – I will *bless* Thee, O Lord....

* * * * *

"I will give thanks to the Lord
With all my heart;
I will tell of all Thy wonders.
I will be glad and exult in Thee.
I will sing praise to Thy name,
O Most High."
PSALM 9: 1, 2

For a Fatherless Child

The Skipper got his Fathers Day cards in the mail this year. His son and daughter live a thousand miles away, and the days when they could just slide up on his lap with a home-made verse or picture are only a memory. But oh, what priceless memories they are! Who can place a value on the time a father spends with his growing children?

The Skipper is a family man, for sure. When he came to Alaska to fish, you can bet he took his kids along. For the first three seasons, they worked side by side with him out on the back deck, cleaning the salmon he brought aboard.

It was there our kids got to know their dad as a man at his work. They cheered as he struggled to bring in the big ones. They felt the disappointment when a nice one got away. They shared the worry in his face when the catch was small. This was serious business, and they sensed that they were a part of it. Looking back now, I can see that this was a time when critically important foundations were laid in their lives.

They say a person's relationship with their father has a whole lot to do with how that person relates to God. If your dad was wise, strong in character, compassionate and loving, that's just fine.

But what if he was mean-spirited and critical? Or fickle and unpredictable? Worse yet, what if he wasn't there at all? A person with a dad like that can store memories and thinking patterns that throw up a real road block.

Thank heaven, God is eternally greater than our memories. Thank heaven, too, that His desire to prove Himself to us as a loving and reliable Father is even stronger than our ache for a "real dad".

So what if Fathers Day has come and gone? God's invitation to heal and comfort a fatherless child stands open every day of the year.

* * * * *

"For my father and my mother
have forsaken me,
But the Lord will take me up."
PSALM 27: 10

September's Song

"Well, Skipper, there they go...." I stood by my husband and watched the jet disappear into the clouds, taking our two young children with it. How I wished we were going home together! But the school year starts before the fishing season ends, and this was just the way it had to be. Grandma and Grandpa would meet them at the other end of the line. They would see to it that clothes were clean and lunches made and pencils ready for the first school day.

Back at the boat, I tried to get on with my day. For once the wheel house was in order. Two little sets of spotless rain gear hung in their place by the cabin door. Inside, two little bunks were made up neat and trim. All summer long we'd tripped over each other, but now a sense of uncrowded quiet settled down over the boat.

That's when I first remember hearing it – the haunting strain of a September Song. It had a touching melody, with verses about growing and changing; about empty nests and letting go. There was much to be done that day, but something in my mother-heart made me stop what I was doing to listen.

Years later, we would watch our children board the plane again. This time there would be no waiting grandparents. No one to help with clothes and lunches and pencils. The kids were grown now, and people were calling them "young adults".

That was the year I would return to the house to find whole rooms emptied out. Silent, uncrowded halls, and endlessly quiet meals. The awful year when September's Song would scream in my ears and tear at my heart. There was so much to do (*Isn't there always?*), but at least for then the music took over, and I could barely move for the sound of it.

Our kids have been gone a few years now. But every September, as I drive down the road past anxious little families waiting for the bus, or walk through the airport among stacks of luggage and hugs and tears, I still hear that song. And looking into the faces of a hundred loving parents, I can tell they hear it, too.

* * * * *

"Blessed be the God and Father of our Lord Jesus Christ, the God of all comfort, who comforts us in all our affliction." II COR 1: 3, 4

Stick and Stay....

"Stick and stay and make it pay,"
   I've always heard the Skipper say.
"The fish come in – one at a time.
   We'll troll the Cape and do just fine."

I'd watch the others pass us by
   With stacks a-smokin', on the fly.
It made me itch to pull and run
   In search of bigger scores – more fun!

I told myself the thing to do
   Was slice our fishing boat in two.
Convinced I'd find a better route,
   I split the hull and started out.

Once at sea in half a boat,
   I tried in vain to keep afloat.
Far off the Cape and out of sight,
   A mayday call went out that night.

I think about what might have been
    If I'd have sailed away back then.
If help had not so soon arrived,
    If married love had not survived.

We marked our silver year today;
    Twenty five years of "stick and stay".
My heart goes out to God and friends
    Who helped us build our boat again.

* * * * *

"For Thou hast tried us, O God;
Thou hast refined us as silver is refined;
We went through fire and through water;
Yet Thou didst bring us out into
A place of abundance."
Psalm 66: 10, 12

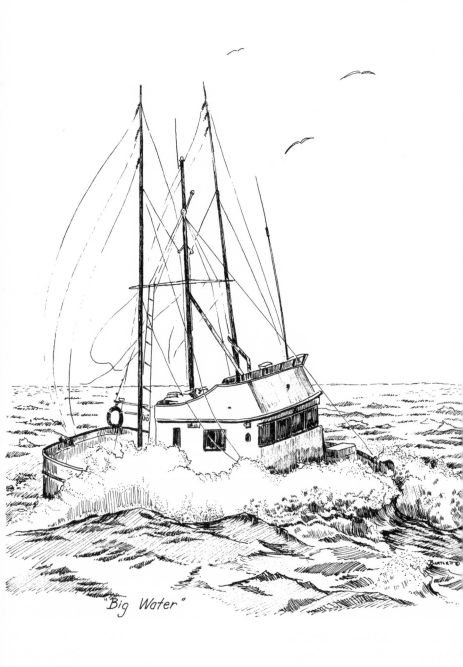

"Big Water"

CHAPTER FIVE

Dark Nights, Thrashing Storms,
and
Little Boats At Sea

There are no atheists, they say, in fox holes. Ask any fisherman and he'll tell you the same could be said of a boat's wheel house in a raging storm. In moments like these, even the most hardened sailor can be heard to cry out, *"Dear God, have mercy on me!"*

Send The Light

You just can't drive over Sitka's channel bridge but what the sight of the local lighthouse will reach right out and grab you. There's something about that faithful sentry that conjures up visions of wild ocean drama – of dark nights and thrashing storms and little boats at sea....

He'd been running up the coastline for what seemed like hours. This was no time for a boat like his to be out on the water! What had started out as a short jaunt to snag a few fish had stretched into a longer day than he'd planned. Now the night swallowed him up in what was turning out to be a hellish nightmare.

A demon wind had screamed in from nowhere, turning the friendly ocean into a spiteful menace. Its mountainous swells lifted and dropped his little craft again and again, while a sharp chop hammered away at its flimsy planks.

Through rain-pelted windows he desperately combed the black shoreline for any sign of a landmark. Where was that inlet? If he missed the turn, he was doomed for sure. For the hundredth time he dragged out his spotlight. Its puny beam disappeared just past the bow, overpowered by the darkness. Finally the young skipper just held on for dear life, waiting for the ocean storm to pronounce its sentence of death.

All hope was gone when he spotted her, high on a rocky ledge. At last! The lighthouse! Her brilliant beam shredded the thick midnight veil, illumining the entrance to the bay. "Turn in here," she urged the desperate sailor. "Come to the light!"

Down through the years, the lighthouse stands as an ageless symbol of hope. Not a weak and puny light, but powerful hope, able to penetrate any darkness. Able to show the way home.

It's no wonder Jesus chose this metaphor to describe Himself. No one knew as well as He just what a dark place the world can be. "Leave the darkness," He urged. "Leave it and come to the light."

* * * * *

Again therefore Jesus spoke to them, saying, "I am the light of the world; he who follows Me shall not walk in the darkness, but shall have the light of life." John 8: 12

Prevailing Winds

"Who asked *him* to come?" While we strained to hear the Blessing of the Fleet, one very obnoxious intruder did his best to disrupt the ceremony.

Even before the first song, I noticed him causing problems. Twice he knocked over the flowers. Then he scattered papers around and tipped over the music stands. A real trouble-maker, he was. Now, as the program got underway, he really cut loose.

From the back of the crowd, he hooted irreverently during the prayers. More than once he edged up to the microphone, drowning out the speaker's words. His disrespect was obvious to all.

People glared and turned their backs, hoping he would go away. Oh, but he didn't. Our unwelcome guest, Sitka's infamous Southeast Wind, blew on relentlessly until the very end. With almost cosmic irony, the noisy rascal exploded while the Scriptures were read:

"And Jesus rebuked the wind and said, 'Hush, be still.' And the wind died down and it became calm..."

I listened to these words and wondered why, since Jesus can control even the wind, He was allowing it to blow and blow on this day. Do you suppose maybe it's because He thought we could use a gentle reminder?

We Alaskans pride ourselves on our self-reliance. Nothing we can't handle, right? But then the wind comes up fast and the ocean turns black. In a flash, we see that our little boats are no match. Perhaps that afternoon God was saying, *Let this strong wind remind you of your weakness – and of My dependable strength on your behalf.*

When the last song died out, people gladly sought the warmth and comfort of home. The fishermen who had come returned to their boats. Back on board, my thoughts turned from *"Precious Memories"* to an uncertain future – the challenge and danger of the coming season. With the sound of the wind still screaming through the rigging, I probably wasn't the only one who echoed the Sailor's Petition.

* * * * *

"Dear God, have mercy on me!
The sea is so wide
And my boat is so small."

Storm Run!

"No way our anchor's ever going to hold in this!" Lazaria Island is usually our favorite anchorage. But on this night, an unpredicted storm had moved in suddenly from the southwest. The water behind the island whipped into a five-foot chop in minutes, and it had the Skipper worried. *"We'd better make a run for town before this gets worse!"*

"So where's town?" I wondered. In the black night, who could tell? The Skipper checked his chart, set the auto-pilot for Vitskari Island, and pulled out into the open water. *"We'll just keep her on this course 'til we see the marker!"*

By now the wind was howling at gale force, and the seas were stacking up fast. Huge waves poured over the starboard railing. The boat rolled sharply, emptying drawers and shelves with a startling crash. It was an angry night, for sure.

The glow from the instrument panel was our only light. The radar showed Kruzof Island somewhere to port, and open water out front. The auto-pilot hummed in steady rhythm, holding our boat true to the course. The Loran silently tracked our location as we picked our way across Sitka Sound.

A long hour later, a small blip finally showed on the radar screen. *"That's Vitskari marker, straight ahead."* I stared hard into the rainy blackness, but saw nothing. "Well, okay, if you say so...."

Sure enough, though, within minutes Vitskari's twinkling marker light came into view. Thanks to the miracle of some trusty navigating equipment, we were safe!

I dread storms. It's bad enough when you know one's coming. But when they hit without warning, that's the worst. Sometimes they come in the form of a sudden illness, or an accident, or a phone call in the night. Before you know it, you find yourself on an unplanned storm run — jerked from your haven, and scrambling in the dark to get your bearings.

Out comes the chart. On goes the radar. "God, where am I? And where are *You?*" In the blackness of the moment comes the glow of His steady reply. Maybe a forgotten verse, an old hymn, sometimes just an inspirational thought to light the way. Peering out into your suddenly darkened world, you can set your course and navigate the storm with confidence. "Well, okay, if You say so..."

* * * * *

"Thy word is a lamp to my feet and a light to my path." PSALM 119: 105

A Storm and a Rock

What a delightful contrast: giant southeast breakers, like salt-water bullies – running, hissing, pounding everything in sight – and a lone midget boat bobbing peacefully, rhythmically at anchor, oblivious to the water's fury. Separated by an island barricade, each played out the afternoon in its own way.

Safe in the little boat's cabin, I could ignore the storm if I chose. And I did! The heat of the stove and the bite of rich black coffee, warm woolly socks and my favorite magazine – these had my attention instead.

Down in the hold, the morning's catch of kings and cohos were cleaned and iced. Rain-soaked coats were hung to dry. Nothing to do now but rest up and wait out the storm behind that big, wonderful rock!

The interruption of a storm, and the shelter of a rock – more than once I've been thankful for both. Somehow our God, awesome and unseen, seems to know when we could use a break and a little extra protection.

* * * * *

"Those who go down to the sea
in ships,
Who do business on great waters;
They have seen the works of the Lord,
And His wonders in the deep.

"For He spoke and raised up
a stormy wind,
Which lifted up the waves of the sea.
They reeled and staggered
like a drunken man,
And were at their wits' end.

"Then they cried to the Lord
in their trouble,
And He brought them out of their
distresses.
Then He guided them to their
desired haven.
Let them give thanks to the Lord
for His loving kindness."

PSALM 107: 23-31

* * * * *

The Radio Dead Zone

"Rusty! Rusty! This is the Sitka marine operator calling the Rusty!"

"Hey, that's us!" I grabbed the radio mike and responded. "This is the Rusty back to the call...."

Silence. The operator repeated the page, apparently unable to pick me up. Frantically, I answered again. Still nothing!

We'd been anchored up in a little cove off South Baranof for several days, cut off from town and waiting out a nasty storm. Our boat was overdue in Sitka, and I knew that people back home were probably beginning to worry. Likely the call was from my parents, but the high, fjord-like mountains surrounding us were creating what is called a radio signal "dead zone". There was no way we could make contact.

Throughout the afternoon the faint call of the marine operator persisted. Out front, the surf continued to roll toward us in high barricades of angry gray. The growing sense of isolation was sharp and uncomfortable. I was new to Alaska. In all my life I had never felt so *alone*, and I didn't like it.

I never have cared much to be alone, and I don't know many folks who do. On the contrary, most people demonstrate a real need to feel connected. We tend to huddle up in small groups of people just like us. We join clubs and buy cellular phones to stay in touch. We're into e-mail and networking.

Now I'm not saying this is a bad thing, necessarily, but did you ever stop to think about the pockets of isolation our little clusters may have unintentionally created? Social dead zones, they are – populated by the people we thoughtlessly exclude.

Be on the lookout for someone who might be feeling left out and alone. (I'll guarantee it, they're out there!) Do what you can to bring down the barriers and make a genuine contact. Share a friendly word or smile. Let them see your face, not your back.

* * * * *

"I was a stranger and you invited Me in. I was sick and you visited me; I was in prison and you came to Me.

"Truly I say to you, to the extent that you did it to one of these brothers of Mine, even the least of them, you did it to Me."
Matthew 25: 35, 36, 40

Queen of Denial

Whenever we get caught off-guard by an ocean storm, I have a personal response typical of many deck-hands: *Let the Skipper handle it!* Head for the bunk, pull the covers up high, curl up tight, and go to sleep. If I'm to die in this place, I reason, so be it. But I'd just as soon not see it coming....

We'd been stuck at anchor for days with a boat-load of aging fish, waiting out an especially stubborn gale. Finally, though, we could wait no longer. The fish *had* to be delivered, which meant we *had* to make a run for it. The Skipper hauled in the hook and slowly nosed the boat into the glowering face of the oncoming surf. I was at the ready, of course, tucked in bed with a pillow over my head for good measure.

We were well into our roller-coaster ride when a rogue wave took us on the side and gave the boat a good jolt. Outside I heard a crash. The hatch cover had broken loose! Someone would need to get out there and tie it down, but quick! Through the feathers, I heard the Skipper holler, *"I need you to take the wheel!"* Who, *me?* My stomach lurched. Surely not!

Reluctantly, I peeled myself off the bunk and made my way to his side. *"Just keep her quartered into the waves, okay? Don't get us into the trough, now, or she'll roll for sure. But don't take 'em head on, either!"* I peered through the window and swallowed hard. It seemed obvious to me then that when you have to look *up* to see the tops of the waves coming toward you, this is not a good thing! If only I could just crawl back to bed and close my eyes.

There is much in this stormy world from which we would want to turn away. Hungry little children. Lonely people. Frightening headlines. When the crest of the waves is higher than the wheel-house, the temptation is to sleep it off. Turn off the news; toss the paper; close the blinds. Let someone else handle it.

But something tells me God hasn't called us to leave the storms to someone else. For each of us, there is a role to play. So don't be surprised when you hear Him say, "I need *you* to take the wheel!"

* * * * *

"Then I heard the voice of the Lord, saying, 'Whom shall I send, and who will go for Us?' Then I said, 'Here am I. Send me!'" ISAIAH 6: 8

Storm Warning

They left the harbor on a cloudless morning in early June. While friends and family wished them well, the young couple steered their new yacht out of its stall and past the breakwater. A silken ocean called to them and so they went, dressed in hopeful smiles and dreams of pleasant adventure.

Once under way, they relaxed and savored the day. There was bread for eating, light wine for drinking, and fantasies to be shared. Now and then, one or the other would comment that life would surely be good to them. Yes, each agreed, they would travel far in their little boat and the water would be smooth as glass, always. (Unfortunately they hadn't known, in the beginning, how quickly things can change at sea. Should someone have warned them?)

Today in the retelling, they wonder aloud when the cloud had come. Neither can recall, but that hardly matters now. It was there – a dark pillar of a cloud (so small at the start!) – looming up from the western sky and creeping their way. They watched the stormy front advance as surely as a farmer's plow, tilling the water's glassy surface in the straightest of lines, leaving it churned and troubled.

There was no time to think when it hit. The cold edge of the wind slipped under their craft and gave it a toss. Food was spilled and favorite things were broken. There was much shouting; they both remember that. Harsh words and angry looks that left them shocked and hurt. (Where, in love's haven, do words like this come from?)

The storm passed as quickly as it came. The wind moved on and the water laid back down. In the silence that followed, two somewhat shaken passengers put things back in order. They were relieved to find the boat only slightly damaged. Little things, easy to fix. No harm done, right?

Neither could bring themselves to say they knew better. Though the boat itself was unharmed, it was apparent that something was undeniably changed. Where was the innocence? The unspoiled communion? If only such things as these were as easily repaired.

* * * * *

"The beginning of strife is like letting out water, so abandon the quarrel before it breaks out."
PROVERBS 17: 14

An Empty Stall

I was saddened to hear,
    On the news yesterday,
That a troller went down
    Just off Shelikof Bay.
All hands aboard were presumed
    Lost at sea,
And I shuddered to think
    That it could have been me.

It's a sobering thought those who work
    On the land
Away from such danger
    Can scarce understand,
But a fisherman lives every day
    With the fact
That when he leaves the harbor,
    He may not come back.

I walked with the Skipper past
    Slip number ten,
Emotions rubbed raw
    As the message sank in.
Another friend gone,
    And one more empty stall;
Another name etched
    On the mariners' wall.

Then I heard (Come to think,
     It was yesterday, too)
That the body was found
     Of a woman I knew;
And, try as I may, I can't seem
     To erase
The specter of darkness
     That she must have faced.

Had anyone known,
     Or did anyone care?
Why hadn't she told us?
     Why weren't we aware?
She sat at her desk
     And we daily passed by,
Not seeing her danger;
     Not hearing her cry.

The fishers will gather together
     Next spring
To honor their fallen
     And hear the bell ring.
But what of the others?
     How many must fall
E're I stop to notice
     One more empty stall?

"Humpback and High Hopes"

CHAPTER SIX

AN OCEAN SCHOOL ROOM

"Consider the ravens," Jesus admonished. *"Go to the ant,"* counseled wise king Solomon. Not a bad idea. There's a lot to be learned about life from close encounters with the animals – whether you happen to be on land or enrolled in a salt-water summer school.

The Devourer

I could tell the Skipper was mad. Gaff in hand, jaw set, he stood with eyes riveted on the trolling pole. *There!* The spring at the top of the pole stretched taut and snapped back, bouncing the huge wood beam like a light sport rod.

"Blast! That's got to be a sea lion!" Sure enough, within seconds a massive brown head broke through the water and flipped its silver prize in the air – a beauty of a coho, fifteen pounds at least.

The pole quivered a little. Good! A fish on the float bag! But before the Skipper could reel in, the spring snapped again. Another one for the sea robber.

You'd think he would have gotten full after awhile. But the afternoon wore on and on with that sea lion just picking off one coho after another, like plump silver grapes.

Over the years, we've come to call this guy the Devourer. We met him long before we came to Alaska. When we farmed hay, he was a ground hog. To the wheat grower, he's a locust. To the merchant, he's a thief. No matter what the setting, you can bet he's going to get some of the crop.

You've probably seen him around, too —
picking away at the edges of your life. The
end result is always the same: a hole in the
wallet, and profits dribbling out on the
ground.

Thank heaven we're not at the mercy of
the Devourer. Sure, he'll take a few fish.
Once in awhile, he'll get 'em all.

But in the long run, God is greater.
Greater than any loss. In the end it's God
who meets our needs, and He's not about to
be beat out by some sea lion. They tell me the
secret is to trust Him — just *trust* Him. And
keep on fishing!

* * * * *

*"Yet even now," declares the Lord,
"Return to Me with all your heart. Then
I will make up to you for the years that
the swarming locust has eaten. And
you shall have plenty to eat and be
satisfied."* JOEL 2: 12, 25, 26

An Ocean Schoolroom

They say the ocean is the best of teachers. If that's so, then perhaps a child is its best student. I'm talking about the children of fishermen – the little people who often find themselves at sea largely by a parent's choice.

Left to their own preferences, these kids might rather spend their summers in town, playing in the back yards of friends, climbing trees, and occupying themselves with the things that ought to concern children. Instead, they wind up enrolled in a salt-water summer school – challenged by lessons that are often all at once boring, frightening, difficult, and delightful.

First, there's the things the Skipper wants them to know. Things like how to quickly clean a fish. The importance of pulling your own weight. How to work without quarreling. You know what I mean – the Grown-up Stuff.

Then there's the things they manage to teach themselves. Stylish ways to wear (?!) a ling cod's head. How to carve a rock star's microphone from a long-tailed kelp. Seven ways to gross out your sister. *Kid* Stuff.

But perhaps the most memorable lessons are those the ocean delivers, up front and personal. Wild and sudden storms that quickly teach every student aboard how to pray. A treasure of sea life (so varied and curious!) that stirs an appreciation of God's infinite creativity. Vast and endless horizons of gray that adjust self-important attitudes. Lessons in humility, patience, and faith. The *Really Important* Stuff.

The ocean's classroom isn't just for kids, you know. But it does require eyes that can still see the unseen. Ears that hear unspoken words. Hearts still willing to believe.

Somehow, little children just seem to be better at this.

* * * * *

"Truly I say to you, unless you are converted and become like children, you shall not enter the kingdom of heaven."
MATTHEW 18: 3

Outside Help

Seagulls are so common in our town we hardly even notice them. But no one could have ignored the commotion they raised out in front of our boat one morning last week.

Half a dozen birds were diving and shrieking, circling tightly just above the water. I ran to the bow and saw that the focus of the uproar was a single gull, fighting desperately with something beneath the water's surface.

As the current pulled the bird closer, I could see a fish hook in its beak. A tangle of long-line gear, tied to the hook, was wrapped around his wing. Every struggle to get loose only resulted in pulling his head under. It was obvious that the poor fellow needed some outside help.

As soon as he drifted close enough, I reached down with a shovel and scooped him aboard. He lay exhausted on the deck while I wondered about the next step.

Up close, I saw that a sea gull is not at all like a gentle farm hen. Ignoring the gaping beak and wild eyes, I slowly unwrapped the gear from his wings and feet. Then my husband snipped the line and easily pulled the hook forward and out. Our little prisoner was free.

I gently set him down on the dock and stepped back. He took off in an instant, soaring a little unsteadily out over the channel, then circling back to disappear into the crowd of sea gulls at the fish plant.

People. Aren't they a lot like sea gulls? So many – so busy – so easy to ignore. Some can really fly! But then there are the others – hooked on one thing or another and struggling just to keep their heads above water. I see them and think, "Wouldn't it be great if I could just reach down and scoop them aboard?"

But then I remember that I'm just a sea gull myself, with more than a few scars of my own. I can flutter around and call attention to their problems, sure. But when it comes to getting the hooks out, I'm afraid what they need is Outside Help.

* * * * *

"Our soul has escaped as a bird out of the snare of the trapper;
The snare is broken and we have escaped.
Our help is in the name of the Lord,
Who made heaven and earth."
PSALM 124: 7, 8

Harlan The Ling Cod

Harlan is a forty-five pound ling cod. He lives a life of relative comfort in an undersea garden on the Pacific coast, many miles south of here. His garden home is a fascinating place, constructed in such a way that visitors are able to peer through a thick glass wall and observe the interactions of the hundreds of marine creatures that live there with him.

The afternoon we toured the garden, Harlan was lounging on the ocean floor— eyes half-closed, just passing the time of day. He looked as satisfied as he could be, content to lay by the hour and lazily watch the other fish swim about. Our guide informed us this fellow's "ling-cod siestas" can sometimes last as long as a week. And all that time, Harlan doesn't move a muscle. He doesn't eat, and he doesn't even really appear to sleep.

The guide went on to describe in graphic detail how once in a great while, as if in response to some internal timepiece, Harlan will shoot up without warning and swallow one of his unsuspecting neighbors whole. He might gulp down another, and maybe even a third! Then, with his belly full of fresh fish, he descends to his watching post to wait until the next time he hears that silent alarm.

Harlan is a classic study in motivation. He demonstrates what the experts have known for a long time: that every deliberate action is generated by a deliberate hunger. That old ling cod might lay there for days on end but when he finally gets hungry enough, he's going to move.

We tend to think motivation is a good thing, don't we? It's what stirs our appetite and rouses us out of bed every morning. It makes us study and work hard to accomplish important and worthy goals.

But it's also possible that in the corners of our minds (often tucked away even from ourselves) we hunger after things that are not so honorable. Harlan's story ought to caution us to spend some time thinking about what it is we really hunger for. Because chances are, sooner or later we'll go after it. It's just a matter of time....

* * * * *

"Blessed are those who hunger and thirst for righteousness, for they shall be satisfied."
MATTHEW 5: 6

A Close Encounter

It was a moment of unusual opportunity. We were anchored in a lonely cove near Point Adolphus, in the dark of an early fall morning. The whales we'd seen offshore the afternoon before had moved in and were now feeding noisily nearby. While the Skipper slept, I sat listening at the galley table. Through the cabin walls, their powerful sounds beckoned me to come closer.

I slid open the door and stepped outside into the pitch black. We were alone in that place. No other boats, no beach cabins, no lights. For that moment, it was just me and the whales. I couldn't see a thing, but I could hear them breathing right next to the boat. Deep, guttural wheezes. Strange sounds of groaning and blowing. The sudden bite of a chilly wind made me shiver.

Just then there was a loud crash. Somewhere in all that blackness, the whales were beginning to breach. The hair on the nape of my neck bristled, and I shivered again. This was not the inspiring encounter I had envisioned! I wanted to stay longer, but it was dark, and I was afraid. Quickly, I retreated into the warm light of the cabin and slid the door shut tight.

It was pitch black on another early morning when Jesus walked across the water toward the boat of a man named Peter. When He was close enough to be recognized, Jesus beckoned the startled man to get out of the boat and come to Him. Peter was a fisherman; he knew that water was not for walking. But by this time in his life he also knew about Jesus, and so he stepped out.

As he made his way through the darkness, a contrary wind came up and whipped at the waves, jostling the boat behind him. Peter heard it, and became afraid. It was then that he began to sink. In fear he cried out, *"Lord, save me!"*

Two unusual opportunities — much different in some ways but in others, quite the same. Both came at the hand of God. Both came in the dark. And in both cases it was fear, blowing in like a chilly wind, that proceeded to drive out faith and cut the miracle short.

* * * * *

"And immediately Jesus stretched out His hand and took hold of him, and said to him, 'O you of little faith, why did you doubt?'"
MATTHEW 14: 31

Stay Behind The Line!

"Okay, okay you guys! Time to get behind the line. Come on... that means you, too! *Behind* the line."

"Aw, come on! We've had the run of the whole ocean all summer – and now you expect us to crowd into that tiny little piece of water and make a living?"

Yes, I'm afraid so. For the trollers it's winter rules, starting October first. If you're going to chase king salmon for the next few months, better plan on doing it in *inside* waters.

Looking out on the horizon, you can see the boats coming – shuffling along like cattle wandering in from summer's open range. Once inside the Sitka Sound corral, they'll behave like any good range cows I've ever seen.

So what's the first order of business? Checking out the fence, of course! Cue up the plotter; scribe a line between Cape Edgecumbe and Bjorka; and then start rubbing that fence. Back and forth, back and forth they'll go, all winter long. Just working that line and working it hard.

Ever wonder what it is about a line, or a boundary, or a rule that draws us to its limits? A person can waste a lot of energy there if it becomes the whole focus. Too much time spent looking over your shoulder. And too easy to compromise. *"Am I over the line? Did I go too far this time? Did anybody see me?"*

My dad had one old range cow who was *continually* at the fence – down on her knees, head turned sideways under the barbed wire, eyes rolled back and tongue stretched out as far as possible for that one choice blade of grass just out of reach.

Meanwhile, out in the center of the field, Dad would be dropping off bales of sweet alfalfa hay for the rest of the herd. That poor old fence rider was missing out!

* * * * *

"Do not be anxious then, saying 'What shall we eat?'... for your heavenly Father knows that you need all these things. But seek first His kingdom and His righteousness; and all these things shall be added to you." MATTHEW: 6: 31-33

Tell-Tale Signs

The rumor spread fast from boat to boat. *The trollers have hit it big at Port Alexander. Better get on down there!* We'd had a skinny season, and so we were all ears. One quick check with the weather channel and we were headed down the outside, hoping to get there by dark.

On our way, we smoked past a couple stray trollers fishing above Cape Ommaney – just a few miles from our destination. *Poor suckers,* I thought. *I'll bet they don't even know there's a hot bite right around the corner.* We rolled on by, anxious to start hauling fish and making some big bucks.

I can't remember today if we caught much at Port Alexander or not. What sticks in my mind about that trip was the sight of those two trollers we'd passed, when they pulled up to the scow the next day to sell their catch.

Both boats had salmon piled up to the rails, loaded down and decks awash. My mouth went dry as I thought of our fast-track run. Come to think of it, there *had* been some whales breaching near those guys. Lots of bait in the water and birds feeding, too – *tell-tale signs of good fishing.* In our hurry to beat the fleet, we'd run right over the bite and didn't even know it!

This story makes me think of a certain Bethlehem innkeeper on a cold winter night many years ago. He'd anticipated hitting it big, too. Travelers were pouring into his town, filling every available room. His till rang crazily as the shekels piled high. The lucky fellow even had a few desperate customers sleeping in the barn.

The next morning, he listened as his guests swapped stories over breakfast. Such incredible rumors they brought to his table! Wild stories of a brilliant star and a sky full of angels. *Tell-tale signs,* they said, *of the birth of a king.* A few were on their way to the palace to check it out.

"I wouldn't mind rubbing shoulders with a king," he thought. "But I have a house full of paying customers to deal with, and a peasant family that's turned my stable into some kind of nursery...."

* * * * *

"For today in the city of David there has been born to you a Savior, who is Christ the Lord. And this will be a sign for you: you will find a baby wrapped in cloths, and lying in a manger." LUKE 2: 11, 12

The Scaredy Cat

Snatched from the comfort of
    Sweet barnyard hay,
Our kitty set sail
    With the family one day.
A maritime feline,
    All furry and wet,
A victim of choices
    (Not *hers*, that's a bet.)

She saw right away
    That this new habitat
Was no place to be
    For an old scaredy cat.
Surrounded by sailors
    And loud engine's roar,
Kitty sneaked off to hide
    In the Skipper's sock drawer.

She only came out
    When she needed to eat,
Then she'd slink, belly low,
    In a hasty retreat.
We never had given her
    Reason to fear,
But she hissed when she saw us in
    Yellow rain gear!

She'd had much more fun
>If she'd just come top-side,
To relax with the others
>Enjoying the ride.
But what dangers might lurk?
>One can only surmise,
When you're seeing the world
>Through a scaredy cat's eyes.

Some folks live their lives
>In a similar way,
Where panic is always
>A hair's breadth away;
Convinced any minute
>Their world could cave in.
And Lord only knows
>Just what might happen then!

Sure, "what-ifs" abound
>On life's journey, it's true.
Can Jesus be trusted
>To carry us through?
When we hear Him call,
>Is it safe to come out?
Hey, there's some things
>A cat need not worry about!

* * * * *

"Peace I leave with you; My peace I give unto you. Let not your heart be troubled, nor let it be fearful." JOHN 14: 27

"Now When I Was a Boy..."

CHAPTER SEVEN

IN IT FOR THE LONG HAUL

The world is full of strong starters. What God really needs, though, is people willing to stick it out for the *long haul*....

Little Things

They told him there was big money to be made in Alaska – tens of thousands of dollars, filling the pockets of folks no better than him. Mountains of gold, they said, and fish as big as Iowa's hogs. Sitting around the fire in his Rocky Mountain cabin, they spun their yarns and he believed them.

He thought back to that evening now as he ran his empty lines for the tenth time in as many hours. Oh, he'd believed them, all right. Enough to sell his cabin and make a down payment on this lousy boat. So here he was – two thousand miles from home and scratching his way through half a season – still waiting for the big score.

A flash of silver snatched him from his reverie. Well, what do you know – the first fish of the day! A scrawny coho, probably worth five dollars at the most. He spat in disgust. Oh yes, big money. Most definitely. For just an instant, he thought of tossing it back. Why mess with it?

Good question, hey? After all, when you're chasing after six figures, what good is a dollar bill? But if our friend is hoping to stay afloat in this business, there's one simple fact he'd better learn quick: In a hook-and-line fishery like trolling, the money comes aboard one fish at a time. And each one is worth something. If he's willing to stay at it, he'll manage to scrape together his first boat payment. Then he'll come back next year and somehow he'll do it again. And again. After ten seasons, he'll have a boat paid for and (I'll guarantee you) a healthy respect for a dollar bill.

I guess it all boils down to attitude, doesn't it? There seems to be a tendency, when your eye is on the Big Thing, to devalue the little thing you hold in your hand.

Still, the truth is, it's the little things that usually come our way. Small opportunities and assignments. A scrawny fish here and there. What we do with these can have a major impact on the final outcome. Do we waste them? Toss them aside in search of something bigger? Or do we see them for what they are: precious seeds from which the Truly Big Things will finally grow?

* * * * *

"He who is faithful in a very little thing is faithful also in much." LUKE 16: 10

Unfinished Business

Someday soon I'm going to write a poem called "Strong Starts and Unfinished Business". It's been kicking around in the back of my mind for awhile now, and I've just about got it all worked out.

The first verse will be about the excitement of new endeavors. Tell me, who doesn't love a fresh start? This very minute there's a whole fleet of fishermen headed for the starter blocks, and I can tell you, each one of them is full of private hope and good intentions. Never mind the low prices and gloomy forecasts. At this stage of the game, faith is strong and all things are possible.

Then I'll introduce the trusty "eighty-twenty" rule. This is the one that says eighty percent of every task is completed in the first twenty percent of the time allowed. What this means is that most of the kings will be scooped up by noon on opening day. Most of the quota comes in on the first set. *Strong* starts, you see?

There will be a verse, too, about the Red Zone. That's the other twenty percent of the job – the part that eats up most of the time. Fishermen say they burn more fuel chasing that last handful of fish than they care to think about. In the Red Zone, you hear words like perseverance, and discipline, and follow-through. Unfortunately, in the Red Zone, you'll also find a lot of good intentions washed up on the beach.

I'd like to close out my poem with a truly inspiring challenge. What needs to be said here is that God takes His work (and ours!) quite seriously, and He puts a lot of stock in a job well done. *"Hang in there,"* He says. *"See it through!"* I have to confess, though, I'm struggling some with this. The problem is, I keep looking at the work-bench of my own life – littered with fits and starts of half a dozen unfinished projects. Maybe I'm not the one to be giving advice in this case.

But then, the poem's not done yet, you see? Like I said, I have lots of notes for it around here (somewhere!), and some workable ideas. Nothing left to do now but slap on a few rhymes and it'll be finished. I'd say it's off to a pretty Strong Start, wouldn't you?

* * * * *

"Take heed to the ministry which you have received in the Lord, that you may fulfill it."
COLOSSIANS 4: 17

Through The Narrows

The old man wished now that he hadn't looked at the photos. There's power in a picture, you know? The full-color image in the centerfold frightened him: sucking whirlpools of white water and three red marker cans, big as freight cars, laid over and towed under by the current's force.

This was Sergis Narrows, the place where water from broad, sleepy channels crowds in to squeeze through a knothole in the rocks. The picture said it all. That water doesn't go through without a real fight.

He hadn't always been afraid of the narrows. But then he hadn't always been *old* either. A younger, stronger man had piloted boats (big ones!) through there a hundred times. When had he stopped? He couldn't remember, really. He only remembered *why*. Little by little, he'd convinced himself it was too dangerous for a man his age to take on that treacherous passage.

Now instead, he spent his days bored and alone, confined by his own fear to the gentle currents of the quiet cove near his cabin.

He leafed through the picture book again. His daughter had sent it last week as a gift. His hand touched her name on the inside cover.

"What am I doing here?" he muttered. "I have family on the other side of those narrows. Grand-kids I haven't seen in years. Maybe it is a dangerous trip, but there's a whole lot of life on the other side!"

As if shoving aside invisible chains, he grabbed his coat and pushed open the cabin door. "What's a little water, anyhow?"

It only took minutes to get the boat ready to go. Before he could change his mind, he fired her up and pulled out into the channel. And for the first time in unnumbered years, somebody's Grandpa pointed the bow south toward Sergis.

* * * * *

Jesus said, "Enter by the narrow gate; for the gate is wide, and the way is broad that leads to destruction, and many are those who enter by it.

"For the gate is small and the way is narrow that leads to life, and few are those who find it." MATTHEW 7: 13, 14

An Island Dream

He knew they were staring. Well, why shouldn't they? He easily piloted his sea-beaten schooner into the fashionable harbor, searching for an empty slip. The old rust bucket *did* look a little out of place. Up and down the rows he went, past well-manicured yachts plastered with teak and brass. The air was filled with the smell of cocoa butter and light wine and Beautiful People.

He noticed his own boat gave off a few smells, too. Old wood and rotten fish, mainly. He hadn't thought of it until now, but he was probably quite a sight himself. Not much water aboard, though, to spare for a bath. A leathered hand dragged across his bristled chin. Maybe he should have at least shaved.

The flutter of summer conversation grew loud and then soft, as he drifted past one group and then another. Each time it was the same – a hundred versions of a similar stage-whispered remark: *"Why is he bringing that thing in here?"* It wasn't long before he started wondering, too.

But then he remembered. His dad had brought him to this island years ago – long before the white yachts had come. Deep in his memory this was the place where *dreams* were born. Visions of a hopeful future for a little boy, birthed in salt water and warm sand, fanned even brighter in the light of brilliant sunsets and driftwood beach fires. The thought of it still reached and stirred him now. This old captain could use a dream, that's for sure. Yes, that's why he'd come.

He hadn't counted on the change, though. How and when had such snobbish refinement crept in? Such chilly pretense? Somehow he doubted there were any dreams left in *this* place for the likes of him.

By now, the harbor people had turned their attention back to more proper things. It would be best if he just moved on. There was another little marina on the other side of the island, anyway. Maybe it would be different there.

* * * * *

"For if a man comes into your assembly with a gold ring and dressed in fine clothes, and there also comes in a poor man in dirty clothes, and you pay special attention to the one who is wearing the fine clothes, and say, 'You sit here in a good place,' and you say to the poor man, 'You stand over there, or sit down by my footstool,' have you not made distinctions among yourselves, and become judges with evil motives?" JAMES 2: 2-4

Grandpa's Faith Line

Billy watched his grandpa lean hard on the thick line stretched over the side of the boat. He had never been long-lining before, and the first black-cod set was just coming aboard. "Sure feels tight, Bill. I'd say she's pretty well loaded up."

"Boy, I sure hope so, Grandpa!" He hadn't said anything, but so far the whole process had seemed to Billy like a lot of hard work and nothing to show for it. They had spent a week getting the boat ready to go, and another week baiting up. Then there was the crew his grandpa had hired, and the bill for six tons of ice.

All this effort and expense, on the hope that they'd catch enough fish to make it pay. To a fifteen-year-old boy, it had seemed a little risky – up until now.

"I see one, Grandpa! Holy cow, he's huge!" Billy leaned out over the water. "Look, here comes another!" One by one, they started coming over the rail – all wet and shiny, black and beautiful! It was a good set, all right, and the hold filled up fast.

Back at anchor that evening, the young boy thought over the events of the day. Finally he just had to ask: "Grandpa, how'd you know where the fish would be?" It was a big ocean out there, and the fish could have been anywhere – or nowhere!

"How'd I know?" The old skipper raised the hatch cover, revealing the bountiful catch. "Well, Billy, I guess I'd have to say it's not really about knowing. It's more about *believing*. And what you're looking at is faith's sweet reward."

The boy's eyes widened. "What? Grandpa, you mean you set your gear and you didn't even have a clue?"

"Well sure, I had clues. Thirty years worth in this water, I'd say." The cover came down with a satisfying thud. "But in the end, it still boils down to this one thing: a guy's got to *trust* those clues enough to bait up and let down the line."

* * * * *

"Anyone who wants to come to God must believe that there is a God and that He rewards those who sincerely look for Him."
HEBREWS 11: 6 (TLB)

Winter Trollers

There's just no getting around it, folks. Summer is *over*. By now, most of the fishing fleet has headed for home. Nobody's out on the grounds these days but a handful of winter trollers.

While their fair-weather buddies are taking it easy in warmer climates, these hardy few will stay at it all winter long, fighting short days and small scores and the meanest weather you'll find on any ocean.

I've been to the harbor on dark, snowy mornings and watched these seasoned fishermen pour hot water over bow ropes frozen solid by the north wind. As they head out for another day, I can't help but wonder, "Why do they do it?"

Some will tell you they need the money, and every little bit helps. But for others, you get the feeling it's not about money at all. Winter trolling, for them, is about *continuity* – about standing in the gap between fall and spring. Between that which is past and that which is yet to be. Somehow the winter trollers sense they have a part to play in the drama of the changing seasons.

I think, sometimes, about the striking similarities between the seasons of the year and the seasons of life. Seems like the older I get, the more I notice it. Mostly I notice how the clock seems to be speeding up!

Remember when we thought spring would never end? And the long, hot summer? But now I see fall whizzing by, and my graying hair reminds me that winter is on the way. There's just no getting around it.

That might explain why I've become increasingly aware of a handful of people around me for whom the winter season has already come. Even though they could be taking it easy, you'll find these "winter trollers" still hard at it – helping out where they can, teaching Sunday School to squirmy little boys and the like. I watch them and wonder, "Why do they do it?" What would you bet it has something to do with continuity.

* * * * *

"O God, Thou hast taught me from my youth; And I still declare Thy wondrous deeds. And even when I am old and gray, O God, do not forsake me; Until I declare Thy strength to this generation, Thy power to all who are to come." PSALM 71: 17, 18

Caleb's Mountain

Caleb was a winter troller — and one of the best. Last I heard of him, he was over eighty years old and still going at it. He never owned a boat. But if you read last week's parable, you know that's not what it takes to wear the name. No, what Caleb owned was a special mountain — and a heart that followed hard after God through the youthful strength of summer, right on through to the dead of life's winter season.

He was forty years old when he first laid eyes on her, nestled like a purple jewel in the hill country of Israel's Promised Land. He'd come from Egypt in the Great Exodus, and he was on a mission to spy out the land.

While others in his troop gawked at the lush grapes and figs growing in the rich river valleys, Caleb studied the skyline. Surely there was fruit to be grown in the high places, too. And so for him it was settled right then and there. *"I want that mountain!"*

Unfortunately, there would be delays. *Big* delays. Frightening reports of giants in those hills stirred up a rebellion in the ranks that ate up the next forty years. All that time, though, while a whole generation wandered and withered and died in the wilderness, God kept one man's vision alive. Caleb had seen the land of promise with his own eyes. He sensed God had a work for him to do, and he couldn't get it out of his mind.

Finally the day came when a new generation left the wilderness and crossed over the Jordan River. And there, among the sea of bright young faces, shone the wrinkled smile of one old man. Caleb watched his youthful companions take to the broad river valleys. He could have done the same, you know. Who would have faulted him at his age?

But Caleb, remember, was a winter troller. And so it was he chose to lift his wintry eyes to the hills. Somewhere deep in his old heart he felt the surge of God's strength, just as powerful as ever. "Now then," he whispered softly, "I'll take that mountain...."

* * * * *

"The righteous man will flourish like the palm tree.... Planted in the house of the Lord, They will still yield fruit in old age."
Psalm 92: 12-14

The Long Haul

"For Sale!" Now that's a placard
You'll find stowed on every boat;
Most skippers have one
         Ready for display.
And once in every year or two
They hang the ol' sign out,
Then take it down and fish
         "Just one more day!"

You'll see these in the harbor,
Running up and down the mast,
Like signal flags they use
         To start a race,
Reminding all who notice
That a lot of folks don't last;
Not everyone who tries to run
         Will place.

You learn to spot the sprinters,
Out to make the easy buck.
It seems we get a fresh batch
         Every year.
They've heard Alaska's stories
And they're here to try their luck;
They give it all they've got,
         Then disappear!

Thank God for Marathoners –
Fishermen who stick and stay,
Who pace themselves on Heartbreak
                    Hill's tough climb.
They're in it for the long haul,
And they're going to make it pay;
The prize is at the *end* –
                    So take your time.

Dear God, I do get tired;
There are days I want to stop
And try some easy living
                    For awhile.
But You are here to give me strength;
We'll make it to the top!
Just run beside me –
                    Mile after mile.

* * * * *

"Let us also lay aside every encumbrance, and the sin which so easily entangles us, and let us run with endurance the race that is set before us." HEBREWS 12: 1

"A Rusty Old Anchor"

BARTLETT ©

CHAPTER EIGHT

REFLECTIONS AT ANCHOR

"Sometimes at anchor,
The questions start coming.
So who made these mountains?
How old is the sea?"

Anchored up in a quiet cove, a fisher's thoughts (and imagination!) can run in almost any direction.

The Tongue And The Rudder

"Behold the ships also, though they are so great and are driven by strong winds, are still directed by a very small rudder, where ever the inclination of the pilot desires. So also the tongue is a small part of the body, and yet it boasts of great things." JAMES 3: 4, 5

A ship's rudder and the human tongue. Now that paints a vivid picture, doesn't it? A massive freighter maneuvering through the world's greatest oceans by a tiny flap – and people like you and me, maneuvered through life by tongues that sometimes flap a little, too.

I understand how a ship's rudder works. A good pilot can move a mighty big boat through the tightest places.

But how many people do you know who are able to maintain that kind of control over their tongues? Not quite so easy, is it? I'm embarrassed to think of some of the words I've heard roll off my lips. (Makes me wonder if there's anyone at the helm at all!)

We all know what it's like to be on the receiving end of a tongue on the loose. Mean or thoughtless remarks can tear at your heart like barbed hooks. They tend to stick with you, too, playing back in your memory a thousand times. Deadly stuff. Who wouldn't agree that we need to bring this unruly member under control?

So... what's a person supposed to do? Remove the rudder? Tie the boat to the cleats and never leave the stall? (Please don't tell me I just need to "try harder". Surely there has to be more to it than that.)

Jesus said it's what fills the heart that inevitably flows out of the mouth. *"The good man out of his good treasure brings forth what is good. And the evil man out of his evil treasure brings forth what is evil."*

So maybe that should be our focus. Instead of strapping down the rudder, maybe we should take a closer look at what's going on in the wheel house.

* * * * *

"Be filled with the Spirit,
speaking to one another in psalms and
hymns and spiritual songs,
singing and making melody with your heart
to the Lord."
EPHESIANS 5: 18, 19

True North

I just spent much of a week reading up on navigation in an attempt to squeeze a parable out of what I thought I knew about marine compasses. My intent was to draw a parallel between True North and spiritual truth. Then I planned to explore the similarities between the compass needle that points north and the means that we have to determine the way to spiritual truth. It seemed like a clever theme.

During my studies, however, I was reminded that the North Pole at the top of the globe (True North) is not the same North Pole that pulls at the needle of my compass. (That's Magnetic North). I also learned that Magnetic North is likely not the same as North on my compass once it's been mounted in the cabin of our steel boat. (That's *Compass* North, okay?)

Furthermore, this "on-board influence", as it's called, is different for every boat. This means it's very unlikely that the Compass North on my boat will be the same as the Compass North on yours, even when we're moored side by side.

To top it off, they say the earth's magnetic field varies quite a bit from place to place. So if I were to set sail on a long ocean voyage, North (True? Magnetic? Compass?) would appear to be in a different location every day! I don't know about you, but that would concern me.

Needless to say, the parable just didn't work out. I still find it comforting to know that there actually is a place out there somewhere called True North. (It kind of has a solid ring to it, doesn't it?) The question is, how do we find it when everyone's needle points in a different direction? No wonder guys like Columbus chose to raise their sights to the heavens and track on something a little more reliable. I think I'm with them. For the really long trips, I'll take *celestial* navigation any day.

* * * * *

Thomas said to Him, "Lord, we do not know where You are going; how can we know the way?" Jesus said to him, "I am the way, the truth, and the life. No one comes to the Father, but through Me." JOHN 14: 5, 6

A Long-Liner's Prayer

Hey Skipper, was that you I heard out on the back deck last night? I could have sworn you were all alone, but the conversation got pretty lively a time or two. I tried to act like I was sleeping, so you wouldn't notice me listening in....

"Well, Lord, that season sure didn't last long, did it? Just a month ago, I was buying gear and hiring green crew. Guess I had some pretty high hopes then, didn't I? I don't know why I do this every year – get my hopes up, looking for the big score.

"Truth is, though, I needed a big score. Last year's taxes still aren't paid, and it looks like the boat payment will be late again. I'm taking a pretty big risk, too, if I don't get some major maintenance done this summer.

"I do have a lot to be thankful for, though. The weather wasn't too bad. No boats down – no injuries. Just a little gear loss. Thanks....

"You know, I really am a lucky guy when you think about it. Who can put a price tag on the things I experienced out there this

year? The whales that came up close, and the northern lights at anchor. The good feeling that comes from a crew working hard together. Bet there's folks in some city somewhere who would give an arm and a leg to do what I do.

"Salmon season's coming up, and they say the coho run looks strong. We'll get by somehow. We always do. You've never let me down yet, have You? Like I said before, thanks a million...."

Gee, Skip, you had me worried for a minute there, especially when I saw the tears. But then you seemed to stand a little taller when you came back in the cabin. I guess everything's going to be okay after all.

Hey, Skipper – was that *you?*

* * * * *

"I sought the Lord, and He answered me, and delivered me from all my fears."
PSALM 34:4

Play It Safe

"Play it safe!" Not a bad motto out on the water, right? Sometimes, though, it can backfire on you....

Competition runs high for a good spot to set your halibut gear. This year, it seems like everybody had the same idea: Get out there early, set your anchor, stake your claim, and wait for the signal. Our boat was one of hundreds anchored up on the starting blocks a day ahead of time. Yes sir, we were playing it safe.

As the hands on the clock inched toward the noon opening, boat motors started firing up. All around us, I heard the clanging of anchors coming aboard. The Skipper went to the bow and started bringing ours in. Suddenly the boat lurched. *"Oh, no! The anchor's stuck!"*

I stared in disbelief as he tried repeatedly to break us loose. Let out slack. Circle the anchor. Reel in. *No way!* It was stuck good! Meanwhile, twelve o'clock came and went. The crew watched in stunned silence as the other boats streaked across the water, dropping buoys and gear at top speed.

In a final desperate move, the Skipper put her in gear and poured the coal to it. The taut anchor cable laid the boat over hard to starboard, dipping the side rail into the water. He quickly backed off the throttle, and the line went limp. Glory to God – we were loose! Luckily, that frantic little episode only cost us ten minutes. It could have been a whole lot worse.

I've always thought of our anchor as a symbol of safety and security. But from now on I'm going to remember that sometimes an anchor can represent things that hold you back. Things like satisfaction with the status quo. Or addiction to comfort. Or fear of taking a risk.

Jesus lived a radical life; not foolish, but radical. He made risky, long-term investments. Sometimes I wonder if He might be calling us to do the same. Play it safe? Not always. Just once I'd like to break loose of my overcautious lifestyle and take a chance.

* * * * *

"Sell all that you possess, and distribute it to the poor, and you shall have treasure in heaven; and come follow Me." LUKE 18:22

Secret Codes

The fishers I've known are a secretive lot;
They play hide-and-seek
    Every time they unload.
You never can tell
    How much fish one has caught,
'Til you get the key
    To the guy's *secret code.*

A code is a secret
    Just shared with the Chosen;
A measure of loyalty,
    Friendship and trust.
(Over the years we've collected a dozen....)
Most skippers will tell you,
    A code is a must.

Scramblers and sidebands;
    Riddles and spies.
Joe codes with Harry
    And Jim codes with Pete.
Funny thing is,
    We're all watching these guys.
They fish side by side
    With the rest of the fleet!

To tell you the truth, I don't code any more;
Who's catching what
    Doesn't matter so much.
My thoughts turn to puzzles
    I've yet to explore –
The things I *can't* see
    Or discern with the touch.

Sometimes at anchor,
    The questions start coming:
So who made these mountains?
    How old is the sea?
Under the blanket of dark northern beauty
The colors press down
    With a bright mystery.

Down in the foc'sle I keep an old Bible;
Somebody's mother
    Once gave it to me.
Turning the pages,
    The code starts unfolding;
I get the feeling I'm holding the key.

* * * * *

"Thus says the Lord who made the earth,
The Lord who formed it to establish it,
'Call to Me, and I will answer you,
And I will tell you great and mighty things,
Which you do not know.'"
JEREMIAH 33: 2, 3

The Rusty Old Anchor

We snagged into an old anchor out behind Lazaria one day last summer. The thing weighed better than a hundred pounds, counting the chain that came up with it. I know one thing – we have a powerful anchor winch on the bow and it was screaming pretty good by the time the whole mess broke surface. The Skipper had his hands full there for awhile, trying to get loose of it.

Now that rusty chunk of scrap iron lays in a heap at the end of our dock, and for two months I've brooded over it every time I walk by. Surely it has a story to tell.

To whom did it belong? And how had it come to lie half-buried in the mud of the ocean floor? The wind is screaming in my ears this very minute. Was it lost in the storm of a night like this?

A picture comes to mind of a hapless fisherman from an earlier time, caught unaware by a southeast gale and fighting for his life. Time and again the anchor cable stretches and jerks, driving the hook deep into the sticky mire. Finally the bolt holding cable to chain and chain to anchor snaps from the strain, sending boat and captain careening toward the rocks of Lazaria's shore....

I think now of all that history tangled in our anchor line, and how my skipper had wrestled to get free. Two generations of fishermen, with the struggles of one passing on and becoming the struggles of the next. Generational bondage, isn't that what they call it? The sins of the fathers visited on the sons. Particular sins that weave through a family tree, creeping like a snake up one limb and then another.

As I ponder the meaning of these things, the melody of a long-forgotten hymn starts to play in my head. (Can it be that God speaks in a song?) *"On a hill far away stood an old rugged cross..."*

A rugged cross? What ever does that have to do with the tangled snare of a rusty old anchor? I follow the illusive trail of this curious pair, only to find it taking me straight toward the very city of the living God.... (To be continued).

* * * * *

"I was in the Spirit on the Lord's day, and I heard behind me a loud voice like the sound of a trumpet saying, 'Write in a book what you see.'" REVELATION 1: 10, 11

The Rusty Old Anchor (Part 2)

Right from the start, there was something about the old anchor that intrigued me. Plucked from the mud of the ocean floor, I sensed it had come with a hidden message. I'm not one given to visions and dreams, mind you, but I swear one day last week that salt-scarred chunk of history broke silence and started to sing. In a voice worn smooth by a million tides, it lured my soul down a timeless path with ballads of ancient sailors and wayward sons; of generational sins and an old rugged cross.

Verse after verse and mile after mile, the trail of the muse wound its way past familiar scenes and on to places I'd never been. Then without warning, it turned sharply upward, seeming to climb straight into the sky. Still the music called and still I followed, all the way up that jagged hill to its lofty crest.

Down the other side, for as far as any eye could see, stretched a broad, green valley. Nestled in the heart of it was a magnificent city, surrounded by splendid walls transparent as glass and brilliant as gold. Somehow I knew, without being told, that this was the place where God lived and that, for me, there would be no turning back.

The sweet sounds that had brought me this far seemed to swell and hover as I walked the last mile to the city gate.

Once inside, I realized that what I'd thought to be a single voice was in fact a multitude of voices, joined together in a single theme. Countless numbers of men and women – young and old, from every nation and tribe of the earth – each telling a similar story of powerful bondage and cosmic struggle and triumphant liberty at the hand of God.

So many were their faces, it was hard to distinguish one from another. But then I caught a glimpse that made me do a double-take. It was the face of a man, and I sensed I knew him well.... (To be continued).

* * * * *

"And I heard, as it were, the voice
of a great multitude
and as the sound of many waters and as
the sound of mighty peals of thunder, saying,
'Hallelujah! For the Lord our God,
the Almighty, reigns.'"
REVELATION 19: 6

The Rusty Old Anchor (Part 3)

What had started out as simple curiosity about an old anchor had turned into a compelling search, leading me along a mystical path to what must surely be heaven itself. There, among a choir of millions, I caught a glimpse of a man I was sure I knew.

Apparently he recognized me, too. I watched as he pushed through the crowd toward the gate where I stood. Yes, the height was the same. Same golden hair; same strong Scandinavian jaw. For all our years together, there could be no mistake.

"Skipper?" First a slight nod, then a smile. Incredulous, my questions came in a tumble. What was this place? And why was he here? For that matter, why was *I* here? The Skipper seemed surprised I didn't know. "You were the one always going on about the 'mystery' of that old anchor," he laughed. "I figured you'd want to see for yourself!"

He motioned toward the gate. I followed my unlikely guide outside and up yet another trail to a gentle knoll overlooking the city. The air grew heavy as we climbed with the smoky-sweet smell of crushed roses and stale ash. The ground around us was littered with chunks of scrap iron. What's this? A garbage dump in heaven?

"Leg-irons," the Skipper explained. Leg-irons? Yes, and so much more. I saw now that the entire hillside was sprinkled with the broken remnants of every form of enslavement ever conceived in the mind of devil or man. The shattered bonds, they were, of a thousand generations.

Just then, the sounds of the heavenly choir drifted over the wall. *"On a hill far away stood an old rugged cross."* Ah, that song again – just like I'd heard at the first! The melody cleared the smoky air like a sweet wind, and suddenly I could see forever, past the stench and the garbage to the top of the hill.

The Skipper had gone on ahead, and I scrambled to catch up. I found him at the summit, leaned peacefully against the massive strength of a rugged wooden beam. And there, at the foot of that cross, lay a tangled heap of chain... and his rusty old anchor.

* * * * *

"Then they will know that I am the Lord, when I have broken the bars of their yoke and have delivered them from the hand of those who enslaved them." EZEKIAL 34: 27

The Old Rugged Cross

On a hill far away
Stood an old rugged cross,
The emblem of suffering
and shame.
And I love that old cross,
Where the Dearest and Best
For a world of lost sinners
was slain.

So I'll cherish
the old rugged cross,
'Til my trophies at last I lay down.
I will cling to the old rugged cross,
And exchange it some day
for a crown.

❁ ❁ ❁ ❁ ❁

EPILOGUE

"An hour is coming when I will speak no more to you in proverbs and figures of speech, but will tell you plainly of the Father." JOHN 16: 25

* * * * *

Like so many photos tossed in a box, the accumulating memories of our Alaskan adventures pile high in tumbled disarray. Once a week, under pressure of a column deadline, I dig around and pull one out at random, hoping to find the stuff it takes to write another parable.

To make a book from this haphazard collection has been something like trying to sort and mount the whole box in one little album. But to see the harbor parables now, grouped in chapters and bound up in a single volume, is to see that, in spite of a very random approach, there's really been just one story after all.

On the surface, this is a diary of a family's very long ocean journey, and their sometimes turbulent transition. But underlying it all, mirrored in nearly every episode, is the story of another journey, unintentionally written into these pages, of my own usually private search for God. A journey in spirit, true, but certainly no less turbulent.

Is there a God? From earliest days I looked into the sky and wondered. As far back as I can remember, I sensed that there was and I longed to be close to Him – to experience in some tangible way His nearness. This hunger of spirit was for me a source of loneliness, even at that young age. And so it was I sought Him out.

Time went on (this journey, too, was long) and on the way, I forgot some things I instinctively knew as a child. I went away to college, and while I was there, I paid good money for a book that told me God had died. No use looking, it said. This God for whom you long is dead.

Soon after, I was all grown up, with a good job, two fine children, and a new home. Things were motoring along pretty well and so, at least for the time being, I left off the search. God was dead, all right – buried under layers of adult sophistication and pretense. My eyes no longer saw Him. My ears no longer heard.

I suppose if I'd been paying attention, I might have seen the dark cloud heading my way. I might have heard the warning. But I was busy playing grownup games when the storm hit – divorce, and then unemployment – blowing in at gale force, and shattering my little small-town world.

When the air cleared, I found myself on a fishing boat pointed north. I suspected (and rightly so!) that things would never be quite the same.

Life in a salt-water summer school has a way of opening your eyes. Alaska's Gulf was for me a dangerous place, with its fickle southeast winds and restless, death-cold seas. For the first time, I knew what it was to feel real, adult fear. Could that be what prompted me to take up my search for God again? Likely so! We had a Bible aboard the boat; anchored up on stormy days, I had time to read it. I kept a journal, too, jotting down my thoughts and observations as I read.

In my reading I noted that Jesus often used parables – starting with simple stories and things familiar to his listeners – as a means of unraveling for them the deep mysteries of the spirit realm. The process was helpful for me, and so on my journey I adopted His pattern.

Is there a God? This time, as I asked the now familiar question, my eyes took in the vast expanse of gray water, and dazzling shoreline peaks framed by the wide night sky. I thought of the soft, thick fur of the playful seal pup I'd seen on the beach. I felt the gold ring on my wedding finger, placed there the day my broken marriage was mended for good. It was just a handful of evidence, I admit, but somehow it locked hands with a speck of faith in my heart. "Oh yes," I concluded, "There surely is a God."

Maybe it's like what Billy's grandpa said. A person has to trust the clues enough to let down the gear and seek Him out. In a way, that's what I did – setting my "faith-line" again and again, following the clues into ever deeper water and bringing in the catch.

This God that exists – does He require anything of me? And if He does, how do I measure up? When I was a child, I had an intuitive awareness that some things were right and some things were wrong, and that God expected me to do the right thing. My conscience was tender then; when I did wrong, I felt bad.

Over the years, however, this too had gotten a little fuzzy. I grew up into a world of adult rationalizations, where guilt was not allowed. "Guilt," wrote one author, "is an irrational feeling. I'm okay – and so are you!" But now in my ocean school room, I knew better and I needed some straight answers. Like the off-shore skipper, I felt compelled to ask: *"So how'm I doing?"* Let's see the score cards.

The more I read and studied, the more a kind of childlike sense of guilt came back. Not a nagging condemnation, like with Lisa ("Not good enough!"), but a persistent *knowing* that I really wasn't doing very well at all. That I'd fallen 'way short. My guilt wasn't a feeling – it was more like a courtroom verdict. Guilty!

Sin, I had learned, is a capital offense. You sin, you die. To fall short is to incur a kind of debt to God, unthinkable in its magnitude and eternal in its consequence.

This, to me, was not good news! Lord knows, I was no stranger to debt. When we borrowed money for our second boat, we had a tough German banker who looked us right in the eye and said, "I want your blood in this!" We were taking on a heavy debt load, and she wanted no misunderstanding – there would be pay-back.

The Skipper started sweating blood right then as he signed the contract, and then again in the wake of two disastrous seasons in a row when it looked like we would lose everything we had. An unrelenting weight, it was, with no reprieve. Over time, she got her money – every last penny. Yes, I knew about debt.

So much for my journey toward God. So much for a feeling of His nearness. If anything, He seemed farther away than ever. What possibly could be done to span the gap?

Once more I went back to my photo box, in search of helpful parallels. Out came two pictures – one, the image of our helpless little seagull, entangled in a snarl of long-line gear. I remembered how all his struggles, too, had been to no avail. It was then the realization came: If I were ever to find my way to God, I was going to need some Outside Help.

The other snapshot was a close-up of that rusty old chain and anchor. More snarls and more struggles, just confirming what I'd already observed. "How very much like sin this is," I had mused, "all wrapped around a life and generally fouling things up." And then a thought occurred to me: Sin will wrap around you like that chain, yes, but it's *the weight of the debt* that will pull you under.

It was the anchor parable that led me to focus my search on the subject of Christianity's cross. What was the connection, I wondered, between the choking tangle of sin, the weight of an unyielding debt, and an old rugged cross? I looked for clues in Jesus' words during the critical days just prior to His death. What kind of stories had He told then that would shed light for me now?

I found it interesting to note that when it came down to the wire in those last days, Jesus stopped teaching with proverbs and parables. This was a time for straight talk. "We're going to Jerusalem," He told His disciples plainly. "When we get there, I'm going to die..."

No room for misunderstanding in that. But it left their minds in a tumble. They'd come to believe that this man they followed was God Himself, come down to set up a sort of heaven on earth. And now God was going to die? Jesus continued:

"...and three days later I will rise again."

We're numb by now to this familiar Easter script, but think of the disciples' confused reaction as they heard it for the first time.

Later, in His last meal before His death, Jesus took the Jewish Passover cup – a symbol of contractual payment for sin – and addressed His friends: *"Drink from it, all of you; for this is My blood of the covenant (contract), which is to be shed on behalf of many for the forgiveness of sins."*

In so many words, He was saying to them, "I've come to *pay your debt!"*

At this point I have to tell you, I have no pictures in my box to which this can compare. What do I know of such things? In my experience, people who die stay dead. And nobody I know is going to pay any debt of mine. The idea that *God* would pay it in full – His blood for mine – is truly without parallel.

If what He was saying were true, however, this would be the Outside Help I was needing: Jesus, my substitute, in an encounter with a criminal's cross, dealing with the tangle of my sin and the weight of my guilt.

Sure enough, just like He said, Jesus went to Jerusalem and met His death. His anguished disciples watched Him die. And sure enough, just like He said, three days later He was back on His feet. This, too, His disciples saw, along with hundreds of other eye-witnesses.

His resurrection, Jesus had said, would be the proof of His claims. Once again in my search I found myself left with a handful of evidence and a choice: to believe and keep fishing, or to pull the gear and give it up.

I read where, at that same last supper, one of the disciples had made a request. "Lord, show us the Father, and it is enough for us." (I'm with you, Philip!) If there is to be no heaven on earth, at least tell us how to get there from here. The response was no less startling than anything else Jesus had said to them lately:

"Have I been so long with you and yet you have not come to know Me, Philip? He who has seen Me has seen the Father. I am the way. No one comes to the Father, but through Me."

Something inside the modern mind recoils at the implications of His words. "Give up your other options," He was saying. "There are none." No other way? As I read this, the picture of the narrows came to mind. And then I thought of that old man, trapped by his fear on the other side. I felt his fear and it made me want to hang back, too. I knew what was being required here.

At the same time, I felt a strange tug at my heart to go on through. It was then I began to see that all the time I'd been seeking for God, He'd been seeking me, too. Ever so faintly, I heard His voice. Go or no-go? In the end, I knew it was my call.

That old anchor stayed on our dock for the better part of a year. Then one day I noticed the chain was missing. Not long after, the anchor disappeared too, leaving nothing but a few traces of rust-stained wood – and a picture in my box I hope I never forget.

* * * * *

* * * * *

"And you will seek Me and find Me,
when you search for Me with all your heart.
And I will be found by you."

JEREMIAH 29: 13, 14

* * * * *

Fish Tales
For Heaven's Sake!

* * * * *

To order additional copies of this book, send $9.95 for each copy, plus shipping and sales tax as indicated below, to the following address:

Mountain Ministries
P.O. Box 6131
Sitka, Alaska 99835

* * * * *

_____ copies @ $9.95: .... $_____

Shipping: .... $_____
(Book Rate: $2.75 for the first book and 75 cents for each additional book. Surface shipping may take 4 to 6 weeks. Air Mail: $4.00 per book)

Sales Tax: .... $_____
Please add 5% for books shipped to addresses within the City and Borough of Sitka, Alaska.

Total: .... $_____

(Make check payable to Mountain Ministries.)

Name: _____

Address: _____

City: _____

State: _____Zip_____

Thank you for your order!